D0883723

FIRST PRINCIPLES
OF NUMERICAL ANALYSIS:
AN UNDERGRADUATE TEXT

BURTON WENDROFF / University of Denver

FIRST PRINCIPLES OF NUMERICAL ANALYSIS: AN UNDERGRADUATE TEXT

ADDISON-WESLEY PUBLISHING COMPANY

Reading, Massachusetts / Menlo Park, California / London / Don Mills, Ontario

This book is in the
ADDISON-WESLEY SERIES IN
COMPUTER SCIENCE AND INFORMATION PROCESSING

RICHARD S. VARGA and MICHAEL A. HARRISON,
Consulting Editors

 Printed in the United States of America. Published simultaneously in Canada. Library of Congress Catalog Card No. 69-16406.

PREFACE

I have taught numerical analysis to undergraduates at three universities. At each of them the traditional numerical analysis course consisted of programming and the presentation of specific methods with little motivation and no rigorous discussion of questions of convergence and error estimation. My feeling was that this was certainly no way to begin the training of professional numerical analysts, nor was it even the right way to give applied mathematicians, engineers, and scientists the tools they would need to obtain numerical answers to their problems. Inevitably, either such problems do not fit a standard format or the answers obtained by standard methods are unsatisfactory. In either case, in addition to an understanding of the problem, an understanding of the structure of numerical analysis is essential if one is to obtain an answer. Most, although not all, of the mathematicians and engineers I have spoken to about this agree with me. This book, then, is an expression of this attitude of mine, and has evolved from lecture notes used in courses given at Brown University, the University of New Mexico and the University of Denver.

The user of this text is assumed to have the usual two-year beginning undergraduate mathematics course. Some of the exercises ask the student to write a program. Rather than insist that each student have a programming language as a prerequisite, I suggest that the course be given in the form of three lecture hours plus one laboratory hour per week, the latter to teach programming and to help the student prepare and run the programs called for. There is enough material in the text for two quarters at that rate.

The subject matter is divided into four logical parts. The first part, Chapter 1, is an introduction to digital computers. The second part, Chapters 2 and 3, presents numerical methods based on Taylor's theorem. The third part, Chapters 4, 5, and 6, presents corresponding numerical methods derived from interpolation. The last part, Chapter 7, discusses the solution of linear systems.

I must express my most sincere thanks to the following people for their support and encouragement: Philip J. Davis, Applied Mathematics Department, Brown University; Julius Blum, Department of Mathematics and Statistics, University of New Mexico; and Herbert J. Greenberg, Mathematics Department, University of Denver.

Denver, Colorado
December 1968

B. W.

CONTENTS

Chapter One

DIGITAL COMPUTATION

DIGITAL COMPUTATION

Numerical analysis is certainly not a new subject, for along with the development of mathematical techniques for the solution of scientific problems there has been a parallel investigation of efficient methods of translating abstract solutions into usable numerical answers. There is now available, however, a relatively new physical tool which has stimulated and redirected research in this subject. This device is the high speed digital computer.

1.1 THE STORED PROGRAM COMPUTER

In order to obtain some understanding of what such a machine can and cannot do let us examine the behavior of a human being equipped with a simple desk computer as he works on the following problem. Given is a sequence of one thousand numbers, x_i, which are measurements taken from some experiment. Because of uncertainties in the behavior of the devices associated with the experiment, it may be assumed that a certain amount of noise has been superposed on the data. A crude way to eliminate this noise is to replace the x_i by their averages in pairs, that is, by the numbers

$$y_i = \frac{x_i + x_{i+1}}{2}, \qquad i = 1, \ldots, 999 .$$

To obtain the y_1 our human computer would enter x_1 on the keys of his machine, transfer it to the adder, enter x_2 on the keys, push the add button, then divide by two and record the result. He would do the same with x_2 and x_3, continuing in this way until the job was done. Each entry of a number on the keys takes about two seconds; the transfer, addition, and division take two seconds; the instructions to perform these operations (pushing the buttons) take a second. Thus, the computation of one average requires seven seconds, for a total of roughly seven thousand seconds or about two hours.

Now, suppose we replace that part of the desk machine which performs the arithmetic operations with a high speed electronic arithmetic unit. The addition and division can now be done in several milliseconds, but the problem will still take five thousand seconds. Merely speeding up the arithmetic operations does not produce much of a saving of time. An additional decrease in computing time can be obtained by connecting a high speed memory to the arithmetic unit. This is a device in which lists of numbers are stored. The arithmetic unit can operate on numbers in the memory, and it can also put new numbers into it. If the access time, that is, the time it takes to read or write a number, is of the order of milliseconds, then the total time for the computation is reduced to the button pushing time, which, however, is still one thousand seconds.

The human computer has become a bottleneck. In order to reduce the computing time by several orders of magnitude, it is necessary to have an automatic button pusher. This is the function of the stored program. In addition to the arithmetic unit and memory, a control unit is provided which enables those two sections of the machine to function together on a predetermined set of instructions or program. The high speed digital computer can now be programmed to do the entire set of averages in several seconds. Actually, modern computers can perform the operations indicated above in microseconds.

Data produced or used outside the machine are normally not in a suitable form, so additional devices called input-output units are needed to transfer information into or out of the machine. Typical input-output units are: punched card reader and punch, printer, magnetic tape unit, cathode ray tube, and camera.

To sum up, the four basic sections of the stored program digital computer are the following.

Arithmetic Unit. Performs elementary arithmetic operations. It can also do certain logical operations, such as comparing two numbers.

Storage Unit. Retains in identifiable or addressable locations information in the form of numbers. The contents of any location can be copied on command without destroying the original.

Input-output Units. Provide communication with outside world.

Control Unit. Coordinates activities of other units and oversees performance of the program.

The physical realization of the abstract device described above can take many forms. Early automatic computers were electromechanical and consisted basically of a collection of switches which could be set in various positions and whose settings could be recognized. An N decimal digit number in such a machine would be represented as the state of a collection of N ten position switches, as in Fig. 1.1. If, for the sake of this discussion, we assume that the decimal point is always at the right, then the collection of switches $(S_N, S_{N-1}, \ldots, S_1)$ in Fig. 1.1 represents the integer 26 . . . 4.0.

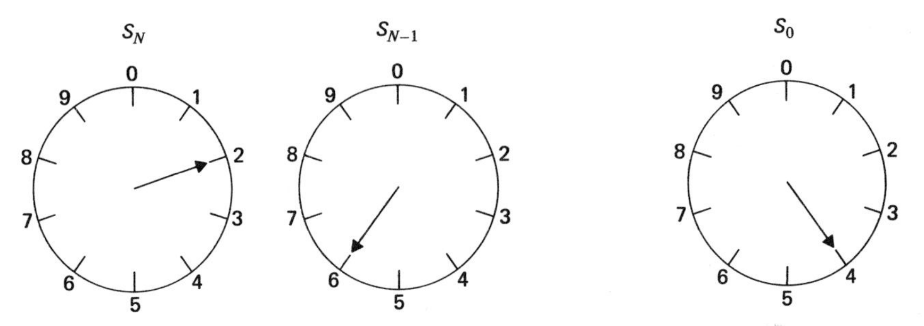

Figure 1.1

Modern computers, excluding input-output units, are electromagnetic, with no moving parts. They use electric or magnetic signals for the storage, transmission, and processing of information. Furthermore, scientific computers usually represent numbers in the binary system rather than in decimal. Recall that if x has the decimal representation $x = a_N a_{N-1} \cdots a_0 \cdot a_{-1} a_{-2} \cdots$, where each a_i is $0, 1, \ldots, 9$, then

$$x = a_N 10^N + a_{N-1} 10^{N-1} + \cdots + a_0 10^0 + a_{-1} 10^{-1} + a_{-2} 10^{-2} + \cdots .$$

Similarly, in the binary system, if y has the binary representation $y = b_N b_{N-1} \cdots b_0 \cdot b_{-1} b_{-2} \cdots$, where each b_i is 0 or 1, then this is a shorthand notation for

$$y = b_N 2^N + b_{N-1} 2^{N-1} + \cdots + b_0 + b_{-1} 2^{-1} + b_{-2} 2^{-2} + \cdots .$$

For example, the decimal integer 5 is 101 in binary, since

$$101 = 1 \cdot 2^2 + 0 \cdot 2^1 + 1 \cdot 2^0 = 5 .$$

Using the binary system, numbers can be represented as a sequence of 2-position switches, as in Fig. 1.2.

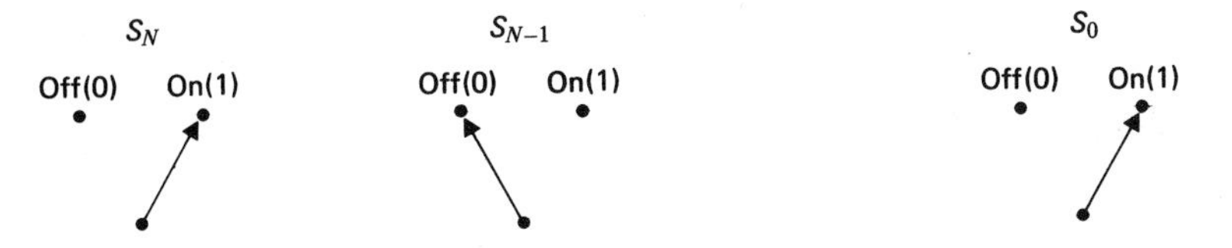

Figure 1.2

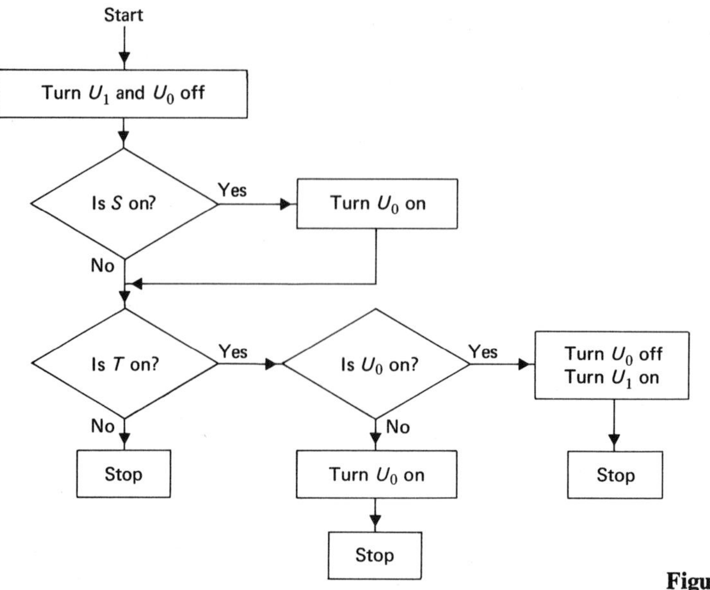

Figure 1.3

S	+	T	=	U_1	U_0		
0		0		0	0	=	0
1		0		0	1	=	1
0		1		0	1	=	1
1		1		1	0	=	2

Figure 1.4

It is not hard to see how a machine which can turn its internal switches on or off and which can tell whether or not its switches are on or off can be used to perform arithmetic. For example, suppose we wish to add the number represented by the single switch S to the number represented by the single switch T and record the result. Two switches will be needed for the result, say U_1 and U_0. Figure 1.3, an outline of the logical steps of the calculation, is an example of a *flow diagram*. It is an unambiguous statement of the logical flow. In this case the reader may check that following the flow diagram will always produce $S + T$ (Fig. 1.4).

1.2 PROGRAMMING

Programming involves supplying a particular stored program for the job at hand. Let us consider what a program for the smoothing problem might look like. Suppose that the numbers $x_1, \ldots, x_{1000}$ are stored sequentially in memory in locations identified by the addresses 101, 102, . . . , 1100. The results will be put in locations 1101, . . . , 2099. The program could be the following list of instructions:

Instruction Number	Instruction
1	Fetch 101

The control unit obtains the contents of location 101, in this case x_1. Associated with the arithmetic unit is a small memory whose locations are called registers. The contents of location 101 are put in a fixed register, say r_1.

2	Add 102

The contents of location 102 are added to the contents of register r_1, the result remaining in r_1.

3	Divide $L(2)$

Here, we have supposed the number 2 has been previously stored in location $L(2)$. The contents of r_1 are divided by 2, the result remaining in r_1.

4	Store 1101

The register r_1 now contains y_1. Control stores contents of r_1 in location 1101.

5	Fetch 102

and so on.

The program could consist of a long list of instructions of the above type. A crucial feature of the stored program machine allows this program to be condensed into a few instructions. This can be done because the program is nothing more than a list of numbers in the memory and as such can be altered by the ordinary arithmetic operations. Each operation the machine is capable of is assigned a numerical code, which is combined with the numerical address to produce a numerical instruction.

More precisely, suppose numbers in the machine consist of ten decimal digits which when interpreted as instructions are split as indicated in Fig. 1.5. If the operation Fetch is assigned the number 0005, then

$$\text{Fetch } 101 = 0005000101 .$$

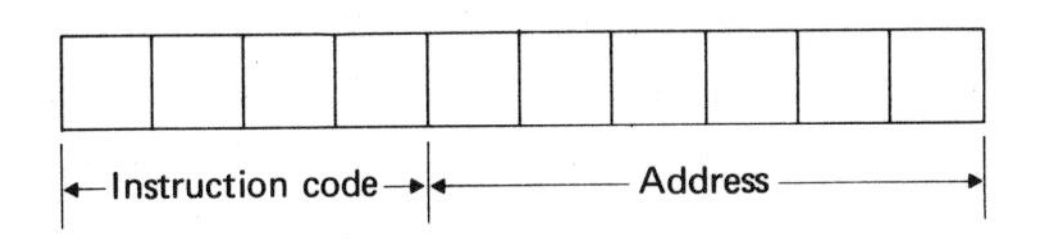

Figure 1.5

Now the instruction Fetch 102 can be formed by adding 1 to the number Fetch 101. The averaging program can now be condensed as follows:

Memory Location	Contents
51	Fetch 101
52	Add 102
53	Divide *L*(2)
54	Store 1101
55	Fetch 51
56	Subtract *L* (Fetch 1098)

Register r_1 now contains the number Fetch 101 minus Fetch 1098.

Memory Location	Contents
57	Branch 68

This is an instruction which we will suppose shifts control to the indicated address if the contents of r_1 are greater than zero, otherwise control continues on to the next instruction.

58	Fetch 51
59	Add *L*(1)
60	Store 51
61	Fetch 52
62	Add *L*(1)
63	Store 52
64	Fetch 54
65	Add *L*(1)
66	Store 54
67	Go to 51

This last instruction sends control back to 51. The above set of instructions forms a *loop*. At the ith pass through the loop the contents of r_1 immediately following instruction 56 are Fetch 101 plus $i - 1$ minus Fetch 1098. Therefore, when y_{999} has been computed, control shifts out of the loop to 68, which could contain an instruction to stop.

The above program occupies much less space in memory than does the program without loops, but it will require more time for its execution because of the address-changing instructions. It should also be pointed out that in order to use the loop program again it has to be reset back to its initial state.

It is useful, indeed essential for more complicated calculations, to have a schematic diagram or *flow diagram* of the steps in the calculation. Such a diagram for the averaging problem for a list of N numbers is given in Fig. 1.6.

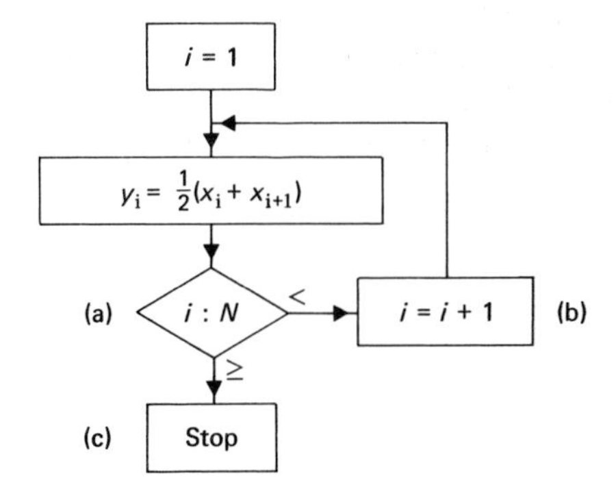

Figure 1.6

Equal signs are interpreted as substitution symbols. Thus, in the first box i is set equal to 1, and in box (b) the value of i is increased by 1. In box (a) i and N are compared, with control proceeding to box (b) if i is less than N, to box (c) otherwise.

The transition from the flow diagram to the machine language is tedious and difficult. Fortunately, the scientific programmer has at his disposal automatic coding systems such as FORTRAN which will handle most of the details of this chore. Using such a system one does not need to know the actual numerical code of the machine, nor is it necessary to know in which locations data are stored. The FORTRAN system translates quasi-mathematical expressions into machine language and also does the necessary bookkeeping. The following is a FORTRAN program for the averaging problem:

```
  DO 1 I = 1,999
1 Y(I) = (X(I) + X(I + 1)) * .5
  STOP
```

1.3 ALGORITHMS

Before the appearance of the stored program computer on the technological scene, numerical methods were designed to fit the constraints of hand computation. Each specific problem had to be studied with great care, and considerable ingenuity was required in order to squeeze as much information as possible out of the conditions of the problem so as to make it accessible to slow hand computation. With automatic computers, however, the tendency is toward automatic methods. For example, one would like to have a program which could calculate the roots of any polynomial, without exception. This is a problem which is still under investigation.

The ideal numerical methods for automatic computers are simple repetitive procedures, easily programmed, and preferably involving only the elementary arithmetic operations. Such procedures are called algorithms [a rigorous definition of algorithm can be given in the language of recursive function theory: see Davis (1958)]. The following example of an algorithm produces as its last step the value of the function

$$a_n x^n + a_{n-1} x^{n-1} + \cdots + a_0 .$$

$$y_{-1} = 0 .$$

$$\text{For } k = 0(1)n$$

$$\lfloor\, y_k = x y_{k-1} + a_{n-k} .$$

All the expressions enclosed by the For statement are to be evaluated for the indicated values of the index taken in order. The indexing equation $k = a(b)c$ means that k goes from a to c in steps of b.

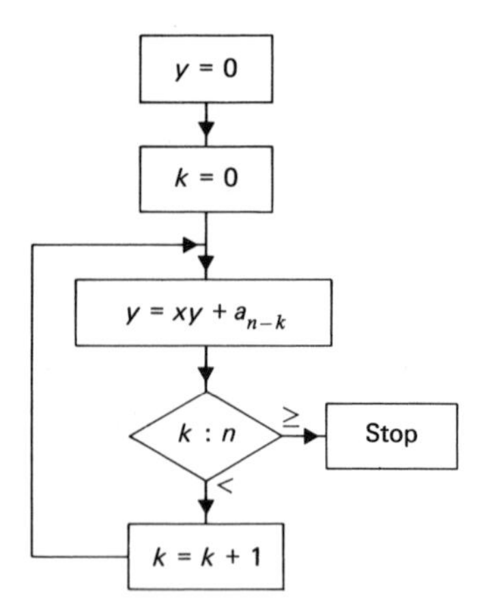

Figure 1.7

A flow diagram equivalent to the algorithm is contained in Fig. 1.7. The fundamental difference between the flow diagram and the algorithm is that in the flow diagram y is no longer an indexed quantity, since there is no need to save anything but the final value of y, which is the value of the polynomial.

By trying a few cycles of the polynomial evaluation algorithm the reader can convince himself that it works, but a proof by induction is also quite easy. For $n = 0$ the algorithm produces a_0, a polynomial of degree 0.

Suppose the algorithm works for $n - 1$. By splitting the algorithm we have

$$
\begin{aligned}
&y_{-1} = 0 \,. \\
&\text{For } k = 0(1)n - 1 \\
&\quad \lfloor\, y_k = xy_{k-1} + a_{n-k} \,. \\
&y_n = xy_{n-1} + a_0 \,.
\end{aligned}
$$

Since by the induction hypothesis $y_{n-1} = a_1 + a_2x + \cdots + a_{n-1}x^{n-1}$ we have

$$y_n = a_0 + a_1x + \cdots + a_nx^n \,,$$

as was to be shown.

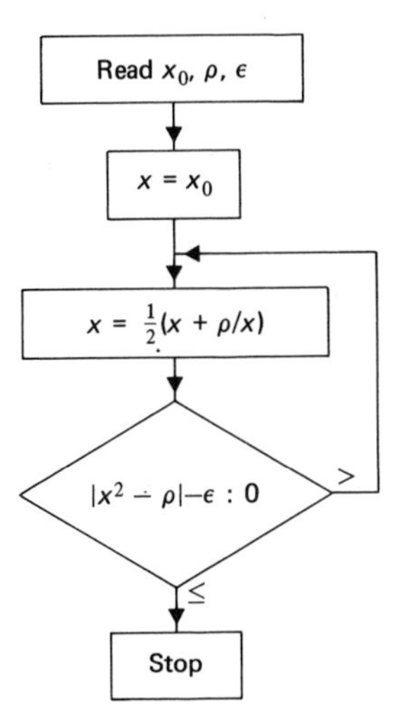

Figure 1.8

Another example of an algorithm is the following sequence for the calculation of the square root of any positive number ρ:

$$x_{k+1} = \frac{1}{2}\left(x_k + \frac{\rho}{x_k}\right),$$

where x_0 must be specified independently. This is an infinite algorithm: the sequence x_k converges to $\sqrt{\rho}$, as will be shown later. To actually use this algorithm, one must include a test which will terminate the iteration when $(x_k)^2$ is sufficiently close to ρ. As in the previous example, in the flow diagram (Fig. 1.8) the iterates are no longer indexed; in addition, it is not necessary to count iterates. We shall present other algorithms as we develop our subject.

1.4 MACHINE NUMBERS

Most of the analysis in this book is based on the continuum of real numbers; however, it is very important that the reader keep in mind that in practice we are dealing with a special, finite set of numbers. Obviously, in a machine with a finite memory only a finite set of numbers can be retained; but even more important is the fact that machine arithmetic operations on this set do not have the same result as the familiar arithmetic operations of real analysis. The following paragraphs will clarify this point.

Most scientific computers have two modes of operation. Integer arithmetic is used for program modification, as discussed in Section 1.2, but for numerical calculation a floating binary number system is used. A *floating binary* number is the couple $(m, \pm f)$, representing the number

$$\pm 2^m f,$$

where m is an integer and f is usually taken to satisfy $\frac{1}{2} \leq f < 1$. f is the *fractional part*, or *mantissa*, and m is the exponent. Each memory location holds a fixed number of bits (binary digits, i.e., zero or one), some of which are allotted to m, the rest to $\pm f$, as in Fig. 1.9. Since m has only a finite number of bits, there is a number M such that $-M \leq m \leq M$.

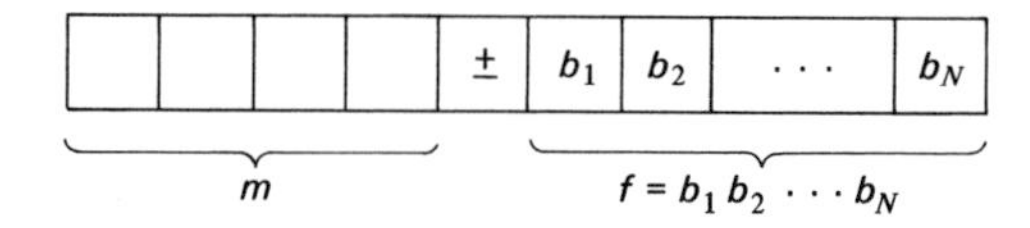

Figure 1.9

Let

$$x_1 = 2^{m_1} f_1, \qquad x_2 = 2^{m_2} f_2.$$

The product $x_1 x_2$ is obtained by first forming the exact $2N$ bit $f_1 f_2$. If $f_1 f_2$ has p leading zeros we set $m_3 = m_1 + m_2 - p$. Let $f = 2^p f_1 f_2$, which is formed by shifting off lead zeros. The fractional part of $x_1 x_2$ is formed by rounding f to N places, usually in the following way: if the $(N + 1)$th bit of f is 1, 1 is added to the Nth bit. Otherwise, no change is made. In either case the next step is to discard all bits beyond the Nth. Call the result f_3. If no overflow $(f_3 \geq 1)$ is caused by the rounding, then

$$x_1 x_2 = 2^{m_3} f_3.$$

If an overflow exists then

$$x_1 x_2 = 2^{m_3+1}(2^{-1} f_3).$$

To form $x_1 + x_2$, suppose $m_1 > m_2$. Let

$$f' = 2^{m_2 - m_1} f_2 + f_1 .$$

We could take $x_1 + x_2 = 2^{m_1} f'$, except that f' may have leading zeros or be larger than 1, but in either event suitable adjustments can be made to bring the sum into the correct form.

The process of addition can cause a loss of trailing bits of one of the terms if it happens to be small compared to the other. For example, in a machine with a ten bit mantissa the number $2^9 + 1.01$ can only be represented by the number $2^9 + 1$. This type of loss of accuracy can produce serious trouble in an automated calculation. Suppose one has a program which generates numbers of the form $y = a + bx + r(x)$ for each x in the interval $[-1, 1]$. The coefficients a, b, and r depend on other parameters. For some values of the parameters the coefficients may have comparable magnitudes, but suppose that for a given parameter set $r(x)$ is small compared to b, and b is small compared to a. If the output of this program is the number $\int_{-1}^{1} yx\,dx$ which, in this case is approximately $\frac{2}{3}b$, the result may be very inaccurate due to the floating addition $a + bx$ and the subsequent loss of bits of b.

The situation described above would be even worse if the program generates a set of numbers $y_i = a_i + b_i x + r_i(x)$, and the output is now

$$\int_{-1}^{1} y_{i+1} x\,dx - \int_{-1}^{1} y_i x\,dx \cong \tfrac{2}{3}(b_{i+1} - b_i) .$$

If b_{i+1} and b_i happen to agree with each other in the first m binary places, and if the addition of a_i to $b_i x$ causes a loss of the remaining figures, then the calculated difference of the integrals will be nonsense.

The mathematician or programmer could get around this difficulty either by somehow separately computing and storing the large and small parts of y, or by the use of multiple precision arithmetic. For the latter, each floating point number is allotted two, three, or more words in memory, thus allowing more binary places to be retained in the mantissa; however, this is an expensive device, since it magnifies both the storage and computing time needed for any problem.

Rounding of products and sums is also a source of error. Predicting the cumulative effect of rounding is one of the most difficult problems of numerical analysis and is beyond the scope of this book. See Wilkinson (1963), Moore (1966).

It is not hard to see that the normal algebraic laws do not hold for machine representable numbers. There are two reasons for this. The first is the finite range of exponents. Suppose we adopt the rule that whenever an exponent falls outside the range $-M \leq m \leq M$ we replace it by M or $-M$, whichever is appropriate. Then

$$(2^{M-1}f_1 \times 2^2 f_2)2^{-2}f_3 = (2^M f_1 f_2)2^{-2}f_3$$
$$= 2^{M-2}f_1 f_2 f_3 ,$$

while

$$2^{M-1}f_1(2^2 f_2 2^{-2} f_3) = 2^{M-1}f_1 f_2 f_3 ,$$

so that clearly multiplication is not associative. It is also true that addition is not associative, and multiplication is not distributive over addition. The second reason these laws do not hold is the rounding process. Consider a machine in which fractional parts of floating binary numbers are allotted three binary places, and consider the triple product $6 \times 5 \times 7$. In floating binary,

$$6 \times 5 = (2^3 \times 0.110)(2^3 \times 0.101) = 2^6 \times 0.011110 .$$

After shifting off the lead zero and then rounding to three places we have

$$6 \times 5 = 2^6 \times 0.100 .$$

Therefore,

$$(6 \times 5) \times 7 = (2^6 \times 0.100)(2^3 \times 0.111) = 2^8 \times 0.111 .$$

On the other hand

$$5 \times 7 = (2^3 \times 0.101)(2^3 \times 0.111) = 2^6 \times 0.100011$$
$$= 2^6 \times 0.100 ,$$

so

$$6 \times (5 \times 7) = 2^8 \times 0.110 ,$$

and therefore

$$(6 \times 5) \times 7 \neq 6 \times (5 \times 7) .$$

EXERCISES

Section 1.1

1. Draw a flow diagram similar to Fig. 1.3 to compute the arithmetic product ST.
2. Given two binary integers, represented respectively by switches $(S_N, \ldots, S_0)$ and $(T_N, \ldots, T_0)$, draw a flow diagram to produce their arithmetic sum. You may assume the machine is capable of all necessary bookkeeping operations. You may also assume the existence of additional switches, if necessary.
3. Draw a flow diagram to find the product of $(S_N, \ldots, S_0)$ and $(T_N, \ldots, T_0)$.

Section 1.3

4. Consider the following algorithm:

$$
\begin{aligned}
&y_{-1} = 0 \\
&\text{For } k = 0(1)n \\
&\quad \left\lfloor\; y_k = 1 + \frac{k}{n-k+1} x y_{k-1} \right. .
\end{aligned}
$$

Use the binomial theorem and the polynomial evaluation algorithm to show that $y_n = (1 + x)^n$.

5. Let $n = a_k 2^k + a_{k-1} 2^{k-1} + \cdots + a_0 2^0$, $a_i = 0$ or 1, and suppose $n \geq 1$. Draw a flow diagram to compute x^n by successive multiplications in which the total number of multiplications is at most $2(k + 1)$. [*Hint:*

$$x^n = x^{a_k 2^k} \cdots x^{a_0 2^0},$$

therefore, generate x^{2^i} by successive squarings.]

Section 1.4

6. Using the example of a machine with a three bit fractional part, show that rounding prevents the associative law for addition from holding. Do the same for the law of distribution of multiplication over addition.

7. Show that rounding alone prevents the associative and distributive laws from holding in an arbitrary finite floating binary computer.

8. Let x_1 and x_2 be the roots of $ax^2 + bx + c = 0$, with $ac \neq 0$. Show that any one of the following three pairs gives the roots of this quadratic:

a) $x_1 = \dfrac{-b + \sqrt{b^2 - 4ac}}{2a}$, $\quad x_2 = \dfrac{-b - \sqrt{b^2 - 4ac}}{2a}$

b) $x_1 = \dfrac{2c}{-b - \sqrt{b^2 - 4ac}}$, $\quad x_2 = \dfrac{-b - \sqrt{b^2 - 4ac}}{2a}$

c) $x_1 = \dfrac{2c}{-b + \sqrt{b^2 - 4ac}}$, $\quad x_2 = \dfrac{-b + \sqrt{b^2 - 4ac}}{2a}$.

Suppose $b^2 - 4ac > 0$. If $b < 0$, which representation for the roots would you use on a floating binary computer? Which would you use if $b > 0$? Why?

Chapter Two

APPLICATIONS OF TAYLOR'S THEOREM, PART 1

APPLICATIONS OF TAYLOR'S THEOREM, PART 1

In this chapter we are going to show that Taylor's theorem with remainder provides a powerful tool for both formulating and analyzing numerical methods for approximating integrals and derivatives of functions.

2.1 TAYLOR'S THEOREM WITH REMAINDER

Repeated use will be made of some theorems from elementary calculus which we now state.

Theorem 2.1 (Intermediate Value Theorem). A continuous function on a closed interval takes on all values between (and including) its maximum and minimum.

Proof. We refer the reader to any calculus text.

Theorem 2.2 (Average Value Theorem). Let $f(x)$ be continuous on $[a, b]$. Let nonnegative numbers a_i be given such that $\sum_1^n a_i = 1$. If $x_i \in [a, b]$, $i = 1(1)n$, then there is a point $\xi \in [a, b]$ such that $f(\xi) = \sum_1^n a_i f(x_i)$.

Proof.

$$\min_{[a,b]} f(x) \leq \sum_1^n a_i f(x_i) \leq \max_{[a,b]} f(x) ;$$

therefore the result follows from Theorem 2.1.

A similar result holds if the numbers a_i are all nonpositive. What is required is that they all have the same sign. The theorem is false if some of the a_i are positive and some negative.

Theorem 2.3 (Integral Mean Value Theorem). Let $f(x)$ and $p(x)$ be continuous on $[a, b]$. Suppose $p(x)$ is nonnegative but not identically zero. Then there is a point $\xi \in [a, b]$ such that

$$\int_a^b f(x)p(x)\,dx = f(\xi) \int_a^b p(x)\,dx .$$

Proof.

$$\min_{a \le x \le b} f(x) \int_a^b p(x)\,dx \le \int_a^b f(x)p(x)\,dx \le \max_{a \le x \le b} f(x) \int_a^b p(x)\,dx\,;$$

therefore the number

$$\frac{\int_a^b f(x)p(x)\,dx}{\int_a^b p(x)\,dx}$$

lies between the maximum and minimum of $f(x)$. The theorem now follows from Theorem 2.1.

The function $p(x)$ could just as well be nonpositive. What is important is that $p(x)$ does not change sign in $[a, b]$.

The next preliminary theorem is Taylor's theorem itself, the proof of which usually goes as follows: Write the identity

$$f(x) = f(y) + f'(y)(x - y) + \cdots + f^{(k)}(y)\frac{(x-y)^k}{k!} + R_k(x, y) \tag{2.1-1}$$

with R_k to be determined. Now differentiate (2.1–1) with respect to y, obtaining

$$\begin{aligned}
\frac{\partial R_k}{\partial y} &= -\frac{\partial}{\partial y}\sum_{j=0}^{k} f^{(j)}(y)\frac{(x-y)^j}{j!} \\
&= -f'(y) - \sum_{j=1}^{k}\left[f^{(j)}(y)\frac{(x-y)^{j-1}}{(j-1)!}(-1) + f^{(j+1)}(y)\frac{(x-y)^j}{j!}\right] \\
&= -f'(y) + \sum_{j=0}^{k-1} f^{(j+1)}(y)\frac{(x-y)^j}{j!} - \sum_{j=1}^{k} f^{(j+1)}(y)\frac{(x-y)^j}{j!} \\
&= -f^{(k+1)}(y)\frac{(x-y)^k}{k!}\,.
\end{aligned}$$

Since $R_k(x, x) = 0$,

$$R_k(x, y) = \int_x^y \frac{\partial R_k(x, t)}{\partial t}\,dt = -\int_x^y f^{(k+1)}(t)\frac{(x-t)^k}{k!}\,dt\,. \tag{2.1-2}$$

When this is stated as a formal theorem we have

Theorem 2.4 (Taylor's theorem). Let f have $k + 1$ continuous derivatives in $[x, y]$. Then

$$f(x) = \sum_{j=0}^{k} f^{(j)}(y)\frac{(x-y)^j}{j!} + \int_y^x f^{(k+1)}(t)\frac{(x-t)^k}{k!}\,dt\,. \tag{2.1-3}$$

An alternative form of Taylor's theorem is obtained by interchanging x and y and then letting $y = x + h$, getting

$$f(x + h) = \sum_{j=0}^{k} f^{(j)}(x) \frac{h^j}{j!} + R_k(x + h, x) , \tag{2.1–4}$$

where

$$\begin{aligned} R_k(x + h, x) &= \int_x^{x+h} f^{(k+1)}(t) \frac{(x + h - t)^k}{k!} dt \\ &= f^{(k+1)}(x + \theta h) \frac{h^{k+1}}{(k + 1)!} \end{aligned} \tag{2.1–5}$$

with $0 \leq \theta \leq 1$, by Theorem 2.3.

When applying these theorems we will usually tacitly assume that the functions involved have as many derivatives as necessary.

2.2 THE RECTANGLE RULE

A simple but useful quadrature formula, or approximate integration rule, can be obtained by integrating Taylor's formula. Since

$$f(x) = f(y) + f'(y)(x - y) + \int_y^x (x - t)f''(t)\, dt ,$$

we have

$$\int_{y-h}^{y+h} f(x)\, dx = 2hf(y) + \int_{y-h}^{y+h} dx \int_y^x (x - t)f''(t)\, dt , \tag{2.2–1}$$

where we have used the fact that $\int_{y-h}^{y+h} (x - y)\, dx = 0$. Thus, an approximation for the integral is given by $2hf(y)$, which we write as

$$\int_{y-h}^{y+h} f(x)\, dx \cong 2hf(y) .$$

Geometrically we have replaced the area under the curve $f(x)$ by the area of a representative rectangle, as in Fig. 2.1.

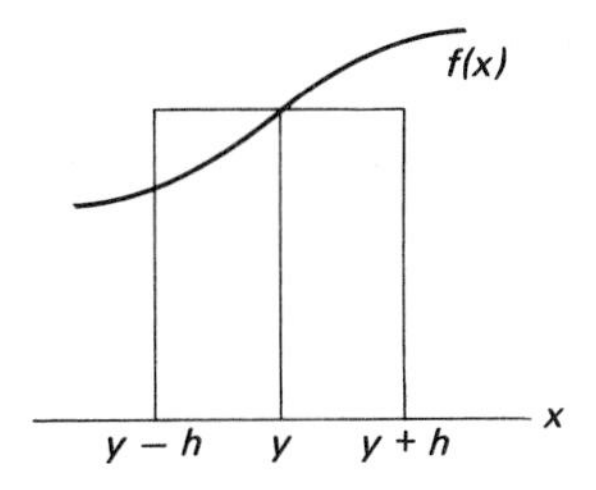

Figure 2.1

The error made in using this approximation is the difference between the exact expression and the approximate one. Calling this error E, we have from (2.2–1),

$$E = \int_{y-h}^{y+h} dx \int_{y}^{x} (x - t)f''(t)\, dt\,.$$

A simple trick can be used to reduce this double interal to a single integral. First, let

$$E_1 = \int_{y-h}^{y} dx \int_{y}^{x} (x - t)f''(t)\, dt\,,$$

and let

$$k_1(x, t) = \begin{cases} x - t\,, & x \le t \le y\,, \\ 0\,, & t < x\,. \end{cases}$$

Then

$$\int_{y-h}^{y} k_1(x, t)f''(t)\, dt = \int_{y-h}^{x} k_1 f''\, dt + \int_{x}^{y} k_1 f''\, dt$$
$$= 0 + \int_{x}^{y} (x - t)f''(t)\, dt\,.$$

Therefore

$$E_1 = -\int_{y-h}^{y} dx \int_{y-h}^{y} k_1(x, t)f''(t)\, dt\,.$$

Since the limits of integration are fixed we can interchange the two integrals, to obtain

$$E_1 = -\int_{y-h}^{y} f''(t)\, dt \int_{y-h}^{y} k_1(x, t)\, dx\,.$$

Applying the definition of $k_1(x, t)$ we find that

$$E_1 = -\int_{y-h}^{y} f''(t)\, dt \int_{y-h}^{t} (x - t)\, dx$$
$$= \int_{y-h}^{y} \frac{(y - h - t)^2}{2} f''(t)\, dt\,.$$

In an entirely similar way, if we let

$$E_2 = \int_{y}^{y+h} dx \int_{y}^{x} (x - t)f''(t)\, dt\,,$$

then

$$E_2 = \int_{y}^{y+h} \frac{(y + h - t)^2}{2} f''(t)\, dt\,.$$

Thus, if we let

$$\lambda(t) = \begin{cases} \dfrac{(y-h-t)^2}{2}, & t < y, \\ \dfrac{(y+h-t)^2}{2}, & t \geq y, \end{cases}$$

then

$$E = \int_{y-h}^{y+h} \lambda(t) f''(t)\, dt .$$

Since $\lambda(t) \geq 0$, we can apply the mean value theorem:

$$\begin{aligned} E &= f''(\xi) \int_{y-h}^{y+h} \lambda(t)\, dt \\ &= \tfrac{1}{3} h^3 f''(\xi), \qquad y - h \leq \xi \leq y + h . \end{aligned}$$

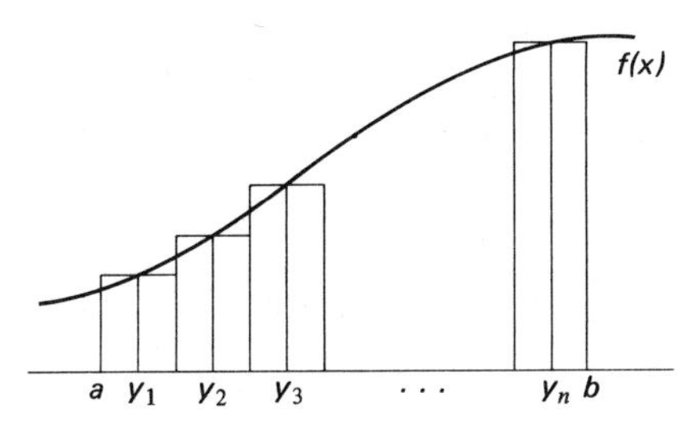

Figure 2.2

The complete rectangle rule for an arbitrary interval $[a, b]$ is obtained by subdividing the interval into n pieces of length $h = (b - a)/n$. Let the midpoint of the ith interval be y_i (see Fig. 2.2). Then

$$\begin{aligned} \int_a^b f(x)\, dx &= \sum_{i=1}^{n} \int_{y_i - h/2}^{y_i + h/2} f(x)\, dx \\ &= h \sum_{i=1}^{n} f(y_i) + \sum E , \end{aligned}$$

where

$$\sum E = \frac{h^3}{24} \sum_{i=1}^{n} f''(\xi_i)$$

with $y_i - \frac{1}{2}h \leq \xi_i \leq y_i + \frac{1}{2}h$. Since $\sum_1^n (b - a)/h = 1$,

$$\sum E = \frac{h^2}{24} (b - a) f''(\xi) , \qquad a \leq \xi \leq b .$$

Note that the rectangle rule is exact, that is, $\sum E = 0$, if $f(x)$ is linear.

2.3 DIFFERENCE QUOTIENTS

Derivatives of functions can also be approximated using Taylor's theorem. For example, since

$$f(x + h) = f(x) + f'(x)h + f''(x + \theta h)\frac{h^2}{2},$$

we have

$$\frac{f(x + h) - f(x)}{h} = f'(x) + f''(x + \theta h)\frac{h}{2}. \tag{2.3-1}$$

The left side of (2.3–1) is called the *forward difference quotient* of $f(x)$. The symbol for the operation of taking the forward difference quotient is Δ. Thus

$$\Delta f = \frac{f(x + h) - f(x)}{h}. \tag{2.3-2}$$

Let us introduce the symbol $O(r)$, where $g = O(r)$ if there is a constant C such that $|g| \leq C|r|$. Then

$$\Delta f = f'(x) + O(h). \tag{2.3-3}$$

Similarly, upon defining the *backward difference quotient*

$$\bar{\Delta} f = \frac{f(x) - f(x - h)}{h}, \tag{2.3-4}$$

we have

$$\bar{\Delta} f = f'(x) + O(h). \tag{2.3-5}$$

The *centered difference quotient* is

$$\hat{\Delta} f = \frac{f(x + h) - f(x - h)}{2h} = \tfrac{1}{2}(\Delta + \bar{\Delta})f. \tag{2.3-6}$$

It is easy to show that

$$\hat{\Delta} f = f' + O(h^2), \tag{2.3-7}$$

for since

$$f(x + h) = f(x) + hf'(x) + \frac{h^2}{2}f''(x) + \frac{h^3}{6}f^{(3)}(\xi_1),$$

and

$$f(x - h) = f(x) - hf'(x) + \frac{h^2}{2}f''(x) - \frac{h^3}{6}f^{(3)}(\xi_2),$$

it follows that

$$\Delta f = f'(x) + \frac{h^2}{6}[f^{(3)}(\xi_1) + f^{(3)}(\xi_2)] .$$

An approximation for the second derivative can be obtained by carrying one more term in the Taylor expansion, as follows:

$$f(x+h) = \sum_{k=0}^{3} f^{(k)}(x)\frac{h^k}{k!} + R_3(x+h, x) ,$$

$$f(x-h) = \sum_{k=0}^{3} f^{(k)}(x)\frac{(-h)^k}{k!} + R_3(x-h, x) .$$

All odd powers of h drop out of the sum of these expressions, giving

$$f(x+h) + f(x-h) = 2f(x) + h^2 f''(x) + R_3(x+h, x) + R_3(x-h, x) .$$

Now, if we note that

$$\Delta\bar{\Delta} f = \bar{\Delta}\Delta f = h^{-2}[f(x+h) - 2f(x) + f(x-h)] , \tag{2.3–8}$$

then using (2.1–5), we obtain

$$\Delta\bar{\Delta} f = f''(x) + h^{-2}\left[\int_x^{x+h} \frac{(x+h-t)^3}{3!} f^{(4)}(t)\,dt + \int_x^{x-h} \frac{(x-h-t)^3}{3!} f^{(4)}(t)\,dt\right] = f''(x) + O(h^2) . \tag{2.3–9}$$

More accurate formulas for f' and f'', and also formulas for higher derivatives can be obtained by inserting the Taylor expansion for $f(x+ih)$ in terms of $f(x)$ into

$$\sum_{i=-n}^{n} a_i f(x+ih) .$$

The coefficients a_i are then determined so that the result is the required derivative with an error term with the desired power of h. For example, suppose we wish to find a five point formula for $f'(x)$ which has an error of order h^4, that is,

$$f'(x) = a_2 f(x+2h) + a_1 f(x+h) + a_0 f(x) + a_{-1} f(x-h) + a_{-2}(x-2h) + O(h^4) . \tag{2.3–10}$$

Since we will need five equations to determine the five unknowns, we must carry five exact terms plus a remainder term in each Taylor expansion, that is, we use

$$f(x + ih) = \sum_{k=0}^{4} f^{(k)}(x) \frac{(ih)^k}{k!} + O(h)^5 .$$

Then

$$\sum_{i=-2}^{2} a_i f(x + ih) = \sum_{k=0}^{4} f^{(k)}(x) \sum_{i=-2}^{2} a_i \frac{(ih)^k}{k!} + \sum a_i O(h^5) .$$

Clearly, the coefficient of $f'(x)$ must be 1, while the other coefficients must be zero, so the equations are

$$\begin{aligned} a_{-2} + a_{-1} + a_0 + a_1 + a_2 &= 0 , \\ h[-2a_{-2} - a_{-1} + a_1 + 2a_2] &= 1 , \\ 4a_{-2} + a_{-1} + a_1 + 4a_2 &= 0 , \\ -8a_{-2} - a_{-1} + a_1 + 8a_2 &= 0 , \\ 16a_{-2} + a_{-1} + a_1 + 16a_2 &= 0 . \end{aligned}$$

The easiest way to solve a system like this is by elimination. If we multiply the fourth equation by h and subtract from the second we have

$$6h(a_{-2} - a_2) = 1 .$$

Subtracting the third equation from the fifth we have

$$12(a_{-2} + a_2) = 0 ,$$

or $a_2 = -a_{-2}$, so that $a_2 = -1/12h = -a_{-2}$. From the third and fifth equations, we get $a_1 = -a_{-1}$ and therefore $a_1 = 2/3h = -a_{-1}$, and from the first equation $a_0 = 0$. Then

$$f'(x) = -\frac{1}{12h} f(x + 2h) + \frac{2}{3h} f(x + h) - \frac{2}{3h} f(x - h) + \frac{1}{12h} f(x - 2h) + \sum a_i O(h^5) .$$

Since the a_i are proportional to $1/h$, $\sum a_i O(h^5) = O(h^4)$.

2.4 SIMPSON'S RULE

The error in the rectangle rule for any arbitrary interval is proportional to h^2. By carrying more terms in Taylor's formula we can obtain integration rules with errors proportional to higher powers of h. For any given function and fixed h these rules may or may not be more accurate than the rectangle rule. All we can say is that as h goes to zero the error will ultimately get smaller than the rectangle error.

To obtain Simpson's rule we write the Taylor expansion to R_3:

$$f(x) = f(y) + f'(y)(x - y) + f''(y)\frac{(x - y)^2}{2}$$

$$+ f^{(3)}(y)\frac{(x - y)^3}{3!} + R_3(x, y) .$$

We now integrate from $y - h$ to $y + h$ to obtain

$$\int_{y-h}^{y+h} f(x)\,dx = 2hf(y) + \tfrac{1}{3}f''(y)h^3 + \int_{y-h}^{y+h} R_3(x, y)\,dx . \tag{2.4-1}$$

If $f''(y)$ were known, we could use the integration rule

$$\int_{y-h}^{y+h} f(x)\,dx \cong 2hf(y) + \tfrac{1}{3}f''(y)h^3 ,$$

with an error given by

$$E = \int_{y-h}^{y+h} dx \int_{y}^{x} \frac{(x - t)^3}{3!} f^{(4)}(t)\,dt . \tag{2.4-2}$$

Using the technique of Section 2.1, namely splitting the x-integration into two parts and then changing the order of integration, we have

$$E = \frac{1}{4!}\int_{y-h}^{y} f^{(4)}(t)(y - h - t)^4\,dt + \frac{1}{4!}\int_{y}^{y+h} f^{(4)}(t)(y + h - t)^4\,dt . \tag{2.4-3}$$

The details of this are left as an exercise.

If f'' is not available we can use (2.3–9). Replace x by y in that equation, solve for $f''(y)$, and substitute the result into (2.4–1), obtaining

$$\int_{y-h}^{y+h} f(x)\,dx = 2hf(y) + \frac{h^3}{3}\Delta\bar{\Delta}f + F , \tag{2.4-4}$$

where by (2.4–3)

$$F = F_1 + F_2 ,$$

$$F_1 = \frac{1}{4!}\int_{y-h}^{y} f^{(4)}(t)(y - h - t)^4\,dt + \frac{h}{3\cdot 3!}\int_{y-h}^{y} f^{(4)}(t)(y - h - t)^3\,dt ,$$

$$F_2 = \frac{1}{4!}\int_{y}^{y+h} f^{(4)}(t)(y + h - t)^4\,dt - \frac{h}{3\cdot 3!}\int_{y}^{y+h} f^{(4)}(t)(y + h - t)^3\,dt .$$

Consider F_1:

$$F_1 = \frac{1}{3!}\int_{y-h}^{y} f^{(4)}(t)(y - h - t)^3\left[\frac{y - h - t}{4} + \frac{h}{3}\right]dt$$

$$= \frac{1}{12\cdot 6}\int_{y-h}^{y} f^{(4)}(t)(y - h - t)^3[3y - 3t + h]\,dt .$$

Let $y - t = sh$. Then

$$F_1 = \frac{h^5}{72}\int_0^1 f^{(4)}(y - sh)(s - 1)^3(3s + 1)\,ds\,.$$

By Theorem 2.3,

$$F_1 = \frac{h^5}{72} f^{(4)}(\xi_1)\int_0^1 (s - 1)^3(3s + 1)\,ds \tag{2.4–5}$$
$$= C_1 h^5 f^4(\xi_1)\,,$$

where $C_1 < 0$. In a similar manner it is easily shown that

$$F_2 = C_2 h^5 f^4(\xi_2)\,, \tag{2.4–6}$$

with $C_2 < 0$. Since C_1 and C_2 have the same sign,

$$F = Ch^5 f^{(4)}(\xi)\,, \tag{2.4–7}$$

for some ξ in $(y - h, y + h)$.

Combining (2.4–7), (2.4–4), and (2.3–8) we have

$$\int_{y-h}^{y+h} f(x)\,dx = \frac{h}{3}\,[f(y - h) + 4f(y) + f(y + h)] \tag{2.4–8}$$
$$+ Ch^5 f^{(4)}(\xi)\,.$$

The constant is independent of f, y, and h, so it can be evaluated by setting

$$f(x) = x^4\,, \qquad y = 0\,,$$

leading to

$$C = -\tfrac{1}{90}\,.$$

To compute $\int_a^b f\,dx$ using (2.4–8), subdivide $[a, b]$ into subintervals $[x_i, x_{i+1}]$, $i = 0(1)n - 1$, with $x_0 = a$, $x_n = b$, $x_{i+1} = x_i + h$, where $h = (b - a)/n$. Assuming that n is even we have

$$\int_a^b f(x)\,dx = \sum_{i=0}^{n/2-1}\int_{x_{2i}}^{x_{2i+2}} f(x)\,dx$$
$$= \sum_{i=0}^{n/2-1}\left\{[f(x_{2i}) + 4f(x_{2i+1}) + f(x_{2i+2})]\,\frac{h}{3} - \tfrac{1}{90}h^5 f^{(4)}(\xi_i)\right\},$$

where $x_{2i} \le \xi_i \le x_{2i+2}$. By the Average Value Theorem,

$$\int_a^b f(x)\,dx = \frac{h}{3}\sum_{i=1}^{n/2-1}[f(x_{2i}) + 4f(x_{2i+1}) + f(x_{2i+2})] - \frac{b - a}{180}\,h^4 f^{(4)}(\xi)\,,$$

where $a \le \xi \le b$. This is Simpson's Rule, with error term.

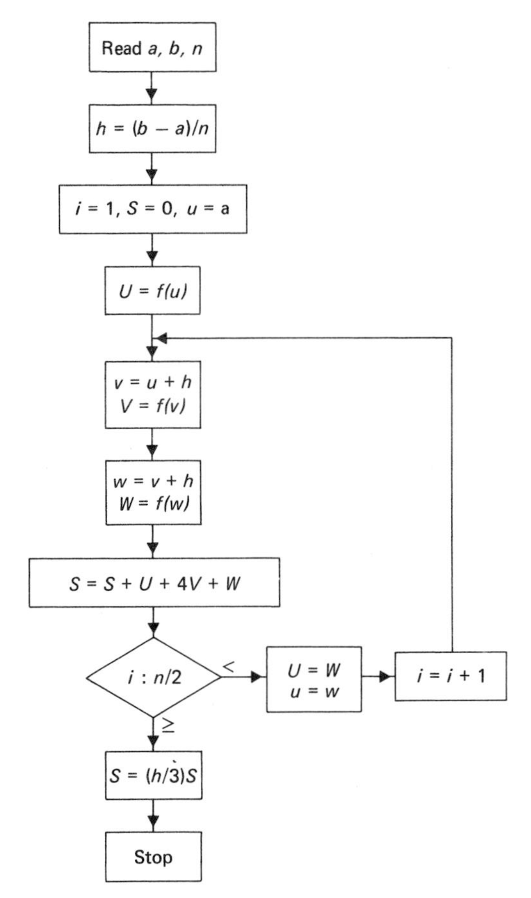

Figure 2.3

Figure 2.3 is a flow diagram for computing an integral by Simpson's rule. It assumes we have some means of computing $f(x)$ for any x. Note that we have kept to a minimum the number of evaluations of the function f without storing the needed values of $f(x)$. Note also the use of variable exits from the $f(x)$ calculation.

EXERCISES

Section 2.1

1. Show by a counterexample that Theorem 2.2 is false if some of the a_i are positive and some are negative.
2. Find a function $\lambda(t)$ such that

$$\frac{f(x+h)+f(x-h)}{2} = f(x) + \int_{x-h}^{x+h} \lambda(t) f''(t)\, dt \, .$$

Section 2.2

3. Prove that

$$\int_y^{y+h} f(x)\,dx = hf(y) + \frac{h^2}{2} f'(\eta)$$

for some η, $y \le \eta \le y + h$.

Section 2.3

4. Find a_i such that

$$f''(x) = \sum_{i=-2}^{2} a_i f(x + ih) + O(h^4)\,.$$

5. Find a_i such that

$$f^{(4)}(x) = \sum_{i=-2}^{2} a_i f(x + ih) + O(h^2)\,.$$

6. Show that

$$f(x + h) - 2f(x) + f(x - h) - \frac{h^2}{12}[f''(x + h) + 10f''(x) + f''(x - h)] = O(h^6)\,.$$

Section 2.4

7. Prove (2.4–3) and (2.4–6).

8. a) Show that

$$\int_{y-h/2}^{y+h/2} f(x)\,dx = \frac{h}{2}[f(y + h/2) + f(y - h/2)] - \frac{h^3}{12} f''(\eta)$$

for some η, $y - h/2 \le \eta \le y + h/2$. [*Hint:* Start out as in the rectangle rule, but use Exercise 2 and the methods of Section 2.4.]

b) Let $h = (b - a)/n$. Show that

$$\int_a^b f(x)\,dx = h[\tfrac{1}{2}f(a) + f(a + h) + \cdots + f(a + (n - 1)h) + \tfrac{1}{2}f(b)] - \frac{h^2}{12}(b - a)f''(\eta)$$

for some η, $a \le \eta \le b$. This is the *trapezoidal rule* with error.

9. Modify the flow diagram in Figure 2.3 so that it will also compute the trapezoidal rule without any additional functional evaluations. Write a program to integrate any given function by both trapezoidal and Simpson's rule. Compute some known integrals.

10. a) The rectangle rule and Simpson's rule are the first two members of a sequence of integration rules. Find the next member. [*Hint:* Carry (2.4–1) to R_5 and use Exercises 4 and 5.]

b) (Optional) Show that the error is $Ch^7 f^{(6)}(\xi)$ and find C.

Chapter Three

APPLICATIONS OF TAYLOR'S THEOREM, PART 2

APPLICATIONS OF TAYLOR'S THEOREM, PART 2

The ubiquitous Taylor's theorem plays a somewhat less direct role here than in the previous chapter, but it does give structure to such diverse parts of numerical analysis as the solution of nonlinear equations, the integration of ordinary differential equations, and rational approximation of functions.

3.1 NEWTON'S METHOD

Newton's method is an iterative procedure for finding a root of a function. Given is some function $f(x)$, and it is desired to find a number α such that

$$f(\alpha) = 0 .$$

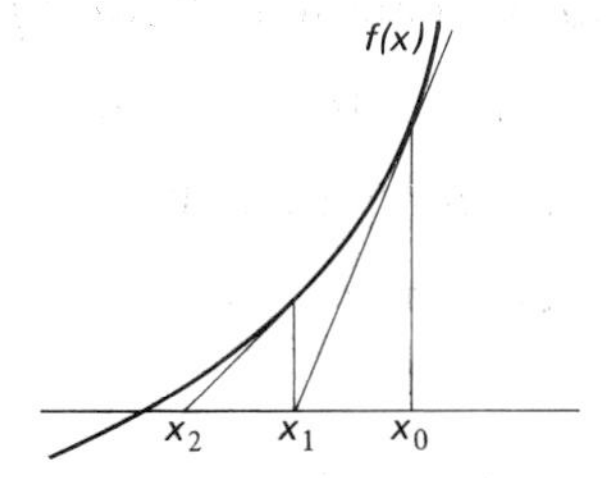

Figure 3.1

Newton's method is pictured in Fig. 3.1. A number x_0 is chosen, the tangent to the curve $y = f(x)$ is drawn at the point $(x_0, f(x_0))$ in the (x, y) plane. The tangent is extended to the x-axis where its intersection defines a new value x_1. The process is then repeated.

Analytically, the iterates x_k are defined by the equation

$$x_{k+1} = x_k - \frac{f(x_k)}{f'(x_k)} . \tag{3.1-1}$$

If we set

$$F(x) = x - \frac{f(x)}{f'(x)}, \tag{3.1–2}$$

then as long as $f'(\alpha) \neq 0$, $f(\alpha) = 0$ if and only if $F(\alpha) = \alpha$. The iteration is now

$$x_{k+1} = F(x_k). \tag{3.1–3}$$

Taylor's theorem provides a means of analyzing the rate of convergence of arbitrary iterations of this type, that is, when F does not necessarily satisfy (3.1–2). We expand $F(x_k)$ about α, getting

$$x_{k+1} = F(x_k) = F(\alpha) + F'(\alpha)(x_k - \alpha) + \cdots + F^{(p-1)}(\alpha)\frac{(x_k - \alpha)^{p-1}}{(p-1)!} + F^{(p)}(\xi)\frac{(x_k - \alpha)^p}{p!},$$

where ξ is between α and x_k. If

$$F'(\alpha) = F''(\alpha) = \cdots = F^{(p-1)}(\alpha) = 0, \tag{3.1–4}$$

but

$$F^{(p)}(\alpha) \neq 0, \tag{3.1–5}$$

the iteration (3.1–3) is said to have *order p*. Suppose there exists an interval J which contains α and all the x_k. For any x in J let

$$\frac{|F^{(p)}(x)|}{p!} \leq M^{p-1}. \tag{3.1–6}$$

Since $F(\alpha) = \alpha$ we have for an iteration of order p

$$|x_{k+1} - \alpha| \leq M^{p-1}|x_k - \alpha|^p.$$

If we define the error of the kth iterate to be

$$e_k = M|x_k - \alpha|, \tag{3.1–7}$$

then

$$e_{k+1} \leq (e_k)^p. \tag{3.1–8}$$

Thus, if the kth iterate is correct to r decimal places, in the sense that $e_k \leq 10^{-r}$, then e_{k+1} will be correct to pr decimal places.

Returning to Newton's method, we have

$$F(x) = x - \frac{f(x)}{f'(x)},$$

$$F'(x) = 1 - \frac{(f')^2 - ff''}{(f')^2},$$

so that

$$F'(\alpha) = 0 ,$$

while in general $F''(\alpha) \neq 0$. Newton's method is of order 2.

In the following pages we give two theorems containing sufficient conditions for the convergence of Newton's method. Before doing so it will be necessary to discuss some mathematical tools. The simplest of these is the familiar triangle inequality

$$|a + b| \leq |a| + |b| .$$

A less familiar form of this inequality is obtained by noting that

$$|a| = |a - b + b| \leq |a - b| + |b| .$$

Similarly,

$$|b| \leq |a - b| + |a| ,$$

so that

$$|a| - |b| \leq |a - b| ,$$

and

$$|b| - |a| \leq |a - b| , \qquad \text{or} \qquad \big||a| - |b|\big| \leq |a - b| .$$

The latter will also be called the triangle inequality.

The next tool is one of the fundamental theorems of calculus, the mean value theorem: if $f(x)$ is differentiable on the interval $[a, b]$, then there is a a point ξ, $a < \xi < b$, such that

$$f(b) - f(a) = f'(\xi)(b - a) .$$

The reader should be familiar with some properties of continuous functions. If $f(x)$ is continuous at a point x_0, then for every $\varepsilon > 0$ there is a $\delta > 0$ such that $|f(x) - f(x_0)| < \varepsilon$ whenever $|x - x_0| < \delta$. If $f(x)$ is continuous at x_0 and $|f(x_0)| < \rho$, then there is a $\beta > 0$ such that $|f(x)| \leq \rho$ if $|x - x_0| \leq \beta$. This follows by noting that

$$|f(x)| \leq |f(x) - f(x_0)| + |f(x_0)| ,$$

so that if $|f(x_0)| = \rho - \varepsilon$, we simply choose β small enough that

$$|f(x) - f(x_0)| \leq \varepsilon \qquad \text{for} \qquad |x - x_0| \leq \beta .$$

Certain properties of convergent sequences of real numbers play an important role in this chapter. A sequence of numbers x_n converges to a limit x if for every $\varepsilon > 0$ there is an N such that $|x_n - x| < \varepsilon$ for all $n \geq N$. A property of sequences which we shall take as an axiom is that every bounded sequence has a convergent subsequence. It follows from this that every bounded monotone sequence (one in which either $x_n \leq x_{n+1}$

for all n or $x_n \geq x_{n+1}$ for all n) has a limit, for let x_{n_k} be the subsequence which converges to x. Suppose the sequence is monotone nondecreasing, i.e., $x_n \leq x_{n+1}$. It follows from the definition of limit that $x_{n_k} \leq x$ for all n_k, and therefore $x_n \leq x$ for all n. Since $x - x_n \leq x - x_{n_k}$, we have $0 \leq x - x_n \leq \varepsilon$ for n sufficiently large, that is, $\lim x_n = x$.

A Cauchy sequence is one with the following property: for every $\varepsilon > 0$ there exists an N such that $|x_q - x_p| < \varepsilon$ for $q \geq p \geq N$. The fact that every Cauchy sequence is convergent provides an important and practical criterion for convergence for it is not necessary to have a candidate for the limit. To prove this, we first note that every Cauchy sequence is bounded. Just take $\varepsilon = 1$, so that there is an N such that

$$|x_q| \leq |x_q - x_N| + |x_N| < 1 + |x_N| \qquad \text{for} \qquad q \geq N .$$

Then

$$|x_n| < 1 + \max_{1 \leq i \leq N} |x_i|$$

for all n. Let x_{n_k} be a convergent subsequence of x_n with limit x. Then

$$|x - x_n| \leq |x - x_{n_k}| + |x_{n_k} - x_n| .$$

By the Cauchy condition if n_k is large enough $|x_{n_k} - x_n| < \varepsilon/2$ for $n \geq n_k$. Since $|x - x_{n_k}| < \varepsilon/2$ for n_k large enough, it follows that $|x - x_n| < \varepsilon$ for n sufficiently large.

Finally, if $f(x)$ is continuous on $[a, b]$ and if $\{x_n\}$ is a convergent sequence in $[a, b]$, then $\{F(x_n)\}$ is convergent and $f(\lim x_n) = \lim f(x_n)$.

We now present two theorems giving sufficient conditions for the convergence of Newton's method. If the curve $y = f(x)$ has the shape shown in Fig. 3.1 it is geometrically clear that the iterates x_k form a decreasing sequence which must converge to the root α. The next theorem gives a rigorous proof of this statement.

Theorem 3.1. Let $f(x)$ be twice continuously differentiable on $[a, b]$. Let $f(\alpha) = 0$, $a < \alpha < b$. Suppose f satisfies the following conditions for $\alpha \leq x \leq b$:

a) $f(x) \geq 0$,

b) $f'(x) > 0$,

c) $f''(x) \geq 0$.

Then if $\alpha \leq x_0 \leq b$, Newton's method converges monotonically to α from the right.

Proof. We will show by induction that

$$\alpha \leq x_{n+1} \leq x_n \leq b . \tag{3.1-9}$$

If $a \leq x_n \leq b$, then by (a) and (b)

$$x_{n+1} = x_n - \frac{f(x_n)}{f'(x_n)} \leq x_n .$$

Now, by Taylor's theorem

$$0 = f(\alpha) = f(x_n) + f'(x_n)(\alpha - x_n) + f''(\xi)\frac{(\alpha - x_n)^2}{2},$$

where $\alpha \leq \xi \leq x_n$. By (c), $f''(\xi) \geq 0$, so

$$0 \geq f(x_n) + f'(x_n)(\alpha - x_n),$$

or

$$\frac{f(x_n)}{f'(x_n)} \leq x_n - \alpha ,$$

which implies that

$$\alpha \leq x_{n+1} .$$

The sequence $\{x_n\}$ is bounded and monotone and has a limit $\bar{\alpha}$. By continuity

$$\bar{\alpha} = \bar{\alpha} - \frac{f(\bar{\alpha})}{f'(\bar{\alpha})}, \qquad \text{or} \qquad f(\bar{\alpha}) = 0 .$$

Since f is strictly increasing, $\alpha = \bar{\alpha}$, finishing the proof.

To apply this theorem, consider the algorithm introduced in Section 1.3 for finding the square root of a positive number ρ:

$$x_{k+1} = \frac{1}{2}\left[x_k + \frac{\rho}{x_k}\right].$$

If $f(x) = x^2 - \rho$, then Newton's method is

$$x_{k+1} = x_k - \frac{x_k^2 - \rho}{2x_k} = \frac{1}{2}\left[x_k + \frac{\rho}{x_k}\right].$$

This $f(x)$ satisfies the conditions of Theorem 3.1.

The next theorem has conditions which are less restrictive on $f(x)$ but it does require a good initial guess x_0.

Theorem 3.2. Let $f(x)$ be continuously differentiable in an open interval containing x_0. Suppose $|f'(x_0)|^{-1} = (1 - \rho)\eta$, $0 < \rho < 1$, $\eta > 0$. Then there exists a number $\beta > 0$ such that if $|f(x_0)| < \beta/2\eta$ then the equation $f(x) = 0$ has a unique solution $x = \alpha$ in the interval $J = [x_0 - \beta, x_0 + \beta]$, and Newton's method converges to α.

Proof. By the properties of continuous functions stated earlier there is an interval $J = [x_0 - \beta, x_0 + \beta]$ in which f' is continuous and such that for x in J, $|f'(x) - f'(x_0)| \leq \rho/4\eta$. Then for x in J

$$\begin{aligned} |f'(x)| &= |f'(x) - f'(x_0) + f'(x_0)| \\ &\geq |f'(x_0)| - |f'(x) - f'(x_0)| \end{aligned}$$

by the triangle inequlaity. Therefore, for all x in J

$$\begin{aligned} |f'(x)| &\geq \frac{1}{(1-\rho)\eta} - \frac{\rho}{4\eta} \\ &= \frac{1}{\eta}\left[\frac{4 - \rho + \rho^2}{4(1-\rho)}\right] \\ &< \frac{1}{\eta}\,. \end{aligned} \tag{3.1-10}$$

Our proof now hinges on the following lemma.

Lemma 3.1. Let u, v, w be in J. Then

$$|f(u) - f(v) - f'(w)(u - v)| \leq \frac{\rho}{2\eta}\,|u - v|\,. \tag{3.1-11}$$

Proof. By the mean value theorem,

$$f(u) - f(v) = f'(\xi)(u - v)\,, \qquad \xi \text{ in } J.$$

Then

$$\begin{aligned} |f(u) - f(v) - f'(w)(u - v)| &\leq |f'(\xi) - f'(w)|\,|u - v| \\ &\leq [|f'(\xi) - f'(x_0)| + |f(x_0) - f'(w)|]\,|u - v| \\ &\leq \frac{\rho}{2\eta}\,|u - v|\,. \end{aligned}$$

Newton's method says that

$$x_{k+1} = x_k - \frac{f(x_k)}{f'(x_k)}\,.$$

We will now show by induction that all the x_k are in J. Certainly x_0 is in J. Suppose x_j in J, $j = 0(1)k$. Then x_{k+1} is defined. Since by definition

$$f(x_{j-1}) + f'(x_{j-1})(x_j - x_{j-1}) = 0\,,$$

we have

$$|f(x_j)| = |f(x_j) - f(x_{j-1}) - f'(x_{j-1})(x_j - x_{j-1})|\,.$$

By Lemma 3.1,

$$|f(x_j)| \le \frac{\rho}{2\eta}|x_j - x_{j-1}|, \qquad j = 1(1)k, \tag{3.1-12}$$

therefore

$$|x_{j+1} - x_j| = \left|\frac{f(x_j)}{f'(x_j)}\right| \le \tfrac{1}{2}|x_j - x_{j-1}|, \qquad j = 0(1)k, \tag{3.1-13}$$

and

$$|x_{j+1} - x_j| \le (\tfrac{1}{2})^j|x_1 - x_0|. \tag{3.1-14}$$

Now

$$\begin{aligned}|x_{k+1} - x_0| &= \left|\sum_{j=0}^{k}(x_{j+1} - x_j)\right| \le \sum_{j=0}^{k}|x_{j+1} - x_j| \\ &\le |x_1 - x_0|\sum_{j=0}^{k}(\tfrac{1}{2})^j \\ &= |x_1 - x_0|\,\frac{1 - (\frac{1}{2})^{k+1}}{\frac{1}{2}} \\ &\le 2|x_1 - x_0|.\end{aligned}$$

But

$$|x_1 - x_0| = \left|\frac{f(x_0)}{f'(x_0)}\right| < \frac{\beta}{2},$$

so

$$|x_{k+1} - x_0| < \beta;$$

that is, x_{k+1} is in J. By the principle of induction all iterates are in J. Then (3.1–14) must hold for all j. Consider, for $q > p$,

$$\begin{aligned}|x_q - x_p| &\le \sum_{j=p}^{q-1}|x_{j+1} - x_j| \le |x_1 - x_0|\sum_{j=p}^{q=1}(\tfrac{1}{2})^j \\ &= |x_1 - x_0|(\tfrac{1}{2})^p\sum_{j=0}^{q-1-p}(\tfrac{1}{2})^j \\ &\le (\tfrac{1}{2})^p 2|x_1 - x_0|.\end{aligned}$$

Since $(\frac{1}{2})^p$ can be made arbitrarily small by choosing p sufficiently large, $\{x_k\}$ is a Cauchy sequence. The limit of this sequence is a zero of $f(x)$, by continuity. There can only be one zero in J, since f' does not vanish in J.

Corollary 3.1. If $|f''(x)| \le M$ for all x, then Newton's method converges if

$$|f(x_0)| \le |f'(x_0)|^2/54M. \tag{3.1-15}$$

Proof. By the mean value theorem $|f'(x) - f'(x_0)| \leq M|x - x_0|$, so that if we set $\beta = \rho/4\eta M$, then $|f'(x) - f'(x_0)| \leq \rho/4\eta$ if $|x - x_0| \leq \beta$. The condition on $f(x_0)$ becomes

$$|f(x_0)| \leq \beta/2\eta = \rho/8\eta^2 M = \rho(1 - \rho)^2|f'(x_0)^2|/8M$$

for some ρ, $0 < \rho < 1$. Replacing $\rho(1 - \rho)^2$ by its maximum of 4/27, we obtain (3.1–15).

As an application consider the problem of finding a nonzero solution of

$$f(x) = \tfrac{3}{2}\sin x - x = 0\,.$$

Since $f''(x) = -\frac{3}{2}\sin x$, $M = \frac{3}{2}$. Examination of a table of trigonometric functions shows that (3.1–15) is satisfied for $x_0 = \frac{3}{2}$. By computing $\beta = |f'(x_0)|/27$, it is easily seen that the computed root lies in an interval which does not contain the origin.

3.2 SINGLE STEP METHODS FOR ORDINARY DIFFERENTIAL EQUATIONS

To begin with, consider a single first order nonlinear differential equation

$$y' = f(x, y)\,, \tag{3.2–1}$$

with initial condition

$$y(a) = y_0\,. \tag{3.2–2}$$

In general, the pair of equations above may or may not have a solution $y(x)$; however, if $f(x, y)$, considered as a function of two variables, is smooth enough then there will exist exactly one solution. To be precise, the following existence theorem holds.

Theorem 3.3. Let $f(x, y)$ be defined and continuous in the strip $a \leq x \leq b$, $-\infty < y < \infty$, where a and b are finite. In addition, let there exist a constant L such that for any x in $[a, b]$ and any two numbers y and $\bar{y}$,

$$|f(x, y) - f(x, \bar{y})| \leq L|y - \bar{y}|\,. \tag{3.2–3}$$

Then there exists exactly one continuous and differentiable function $y(x)$ satisfying (3.2–1) and (3.2–2).

Proofs of this theorem can be found in Coddington and Levinson (1955) or Henrici (1962a). It is sufficient for our purposes to assume the truth of this theorem.

Condition (3.2–3) is called a Lipschitz condition. It holds for example if $\partial f/\partial y$ is bounded, for then by the mean value theorem

$$|f(x, y) - f(x, \bar{y})| \leq \left|\frac{\partial f}{\partial y}\right| |y - \bar{y}| \,.$$

In general, if $f(x, y)$ has derivatives of sufficiently high order so will $y(x)$. We will suppose in the following that $y(x)$ is as differentiable as is needed.

The numerical methods we shall discuss in this book for the solution of (3.2–1), (3.2–2) are called *discrete variable* methods. We choose an integer N and define the step size

$$h = \frac{b - a}{N} \,.$$

We now introduce *mesh points* x_n, where $x_0 = a$, $x_n = x_{n-1} + h$, $n = 1(1)N$ and we seek numbers Y_n which are to be used as approximate values for $y_n \equiv y(x_n)$. See Fig. 3.2.

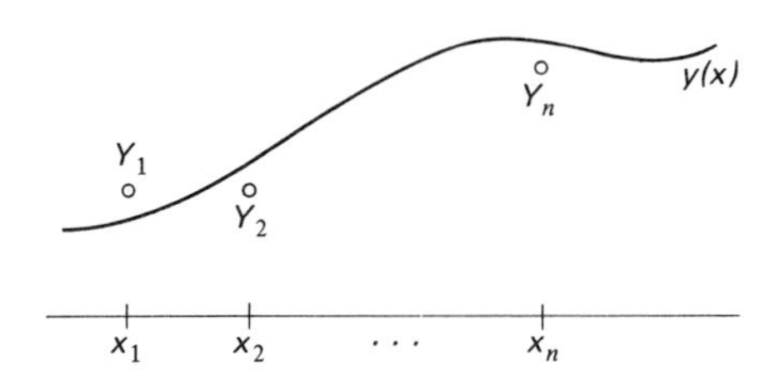

Figure 3.2

The simplest discrete variable method is Euler's method:

$$Y_{n+1} = Y_n + hf(x_n, Y_n) \,, \qquad (3.2\text{–}4)$$

$$Y_0 = y_0 \,.$$

This is obtained by replacing y' in (3.2–1) by the forward difference quotient. Indeed, in Section 2.3 we saw that

$$y_{n+1} = y_n + hf(x_n, y_n) + O(h^2) \qquad (3.2\text{–}5)$$

so that we may think of (3.2–4) as being obtained from (3.2–5) by throwing away the unknown error term $O(h^2)$ and replacing y by Y.

Euler's method is an *explicit single step method* in the sense that Y_{n+1} is explicitly defined by a function which depends only on the previous value Y_n, not on any other Y's. A general single step method has the form

$$Y_{n+1} = Y_n + h\Phi(x_n, Y_n) \,, \qquad (3.2\text{–}6)$$

where Φ is some predetermined function. If

$$y_{n+1} = y_n + h\Phi(x_n, y_n) + O(h^{p+1}) , \tag{3.2–7}$$

the particular single step method is said to have order p. The term $O(h^{p+1})$ in (3.2–7) is called the *truncation error* of the method.

Euler's method has order one. To obtain a method of order two, we first note that

$$\begin{aligned} y_{n+1} &= y_n + hy'_n + \frac{h^2}{2} y''_n + O(h^3) \\ &= y_n + hf(x_n, y_n) + \frac{h^2}{2} \frac{df}{dx}(x_n, y_n) + O(h^3) . \end{aligned} \tag{3.2–8}$$

The presence of df/dx above is awkward. It can be eliminated by using a special case of Taylor's theorem in two variables.

Lemma 3.2

$$f(x+h, y+\tau h) = f(x, y) + h\frac{\partial f(x, y)}{\partial x} + \tau h\frac{\partial f(x, y)}{\partial y} + O(h^2) .$$

Proof. Let $F(t) = f(x + th, y + t\tau h)$. Then

$$F(1) = F(0) + F'(0) + \tfrac{1}{2}F''(\xi) , \qquad 0 < \xi < 1 ,$$

or, using the chain rule,

$$f(x+h, y+\tau h) = f(x, y) + h\frac{\partial f(x, y)}{\partial x} + \tau h\frac{\partial f(x, y)}{\partial y} + \frac{1}{2}F''(\xi) .$$

But by the chain rule again,

$$F'' = h^2\frac{\partial^2 f}{\partial x^2} + 2\tau h^2\frac{\partial^2 f}{\partial x\, \partial y} + \tau^2 h^2\frac{\partial^2 f}{\partial y^2} = O(h^2) .$$

It follows from Lemma 3.2 that

$$\begin{aligned} f(x_{n+1}, y_n + hf(x_n, y_n)) &= f(x_n, y_n) + h\frac{\partial f}{\partial x}(x_n, y_n) \\ &\quad + hf(x_n, y_n)\frac{\partial f}{\partial y}(x_n, y_n) + O(h^2) \\ &= f(x_n, y_n) + h\frac{df}{dx}(x_n, y_n) + O(h^2) . \end{aligned}$$

Solving the above for df/dx and substituting the result into (3.2–8) we have

$$\begin{aligned} y_{n+1} &= y_n + \frac{h}{2}\{f(x_n, y_n) + f[x_{n+1}, y_n + hf(x_n, y_n)]\} + O(h^3) \\ &= y_n + h\Phi(x_n, y_n) + O(h^3) , \end{aligned}$$

where now

$$\Phi = \tfrac{1}{2}\{f(x_n, y_n) + f[x_{n+1}, y_n + hf(x_n, y_n)]\} .$$

This second order method is called *Heun's method.*

Single step methods of higher order are known as Runge-Kutta methods. An example of such is the following method of order four:

$$\Phi(x, y) = \tfrac{1}{6}[k_1 + 2k_2 + 2k_3 + k_4] ,$$

where

$$k_1 = f(x, y) ,$$

$$k_2 = f\left(x + \frac{h}{2}, y + \frac{h}{2} k_1\right) ,$$

$$k_3 = f\left(x + \frac{h}{2}, y + \frac{h}{2} k_2\right) ,$$

$$k_4 = f(x + h, y + hk_3) .$$

Establishing the order of Runge-Kutta methods is quite difficult. The analysis can be found in Henrici (1962a) or Ince (1944).

We now take up the question of the convergence of single step methods. We shall show that the set of numbers Y_i approximates the set of numbers y_i. To be precise, we shall demonstrate that if (3.2–6) and (3.2–7) hold, then

$$\max_{0 \le n \le N} |y_n - Y_n| \le Ch^p , \qquad (3.2\text{–}9)$$

from which it follows that

$$\lim_{h \to 0} \left[\max_{0 \le n \le N} |y_n - Y_n| \right] = 0 .$$

To prove this, substract (3.2–6) from (3.2–7) and apply the triangle inequality to get

$$|y_{n+1} - Y_{n+1}| \le |y_n - Y_n| + h|\Phi(x_n, y_n) - \Phi(x_n, Y_n)| + Ah^{p+1} \qquad (3.2\text{–}10)$$

for some positive constant A.

This inequality is unmanageable; however, if we assume that Φ satisfies a Lipschitz condition, that is,

$$|\Phi(x_n, y_n) - \Phi(x_n, Y_n)| \le L|y_n - Y_n| , \qquad (3.2\text{–}11)$$

and if we let $e_n = |y_n - Y_n|$, then (3.2–10) becomes

$$e_{n+1} \le e_n + hLe_n + Ah^{p+1} . \qquad (3.2\text{–}12)$$

We can now deduce an upper bound for all the e_n by a process known as majorization: Suppose there exist quantities q_n such that $q_0 = e_0$, and

$$q_{n+1} = (1 + hL)q_n + Ah^{p+1}. \tag{3.2–13}$$

Then

$$q_{n+1} - e_{n+1} \geq (1 + hL)(q_n - e_n).$$

Since $q_0 = e_0$, a simple induction shows that

$$q_{n+1} \geq e_{n+1}.$$

In other words, the solution of the inequality (3.2–12) is *majorized* by the solution of the equality (3.2–13).

Equation (3.2–13) is a *linear difference equation* and is solved as follows. We first set $q_n = \lambda$ for all n, which implies that

$$\lambda = -\frac{A}{L} h^p.$$

This is a particular solution of the difference equation. It does not satisfy the initial condition $q_0 = e_0$. We now solve the equation

$$p_{n+1} = (1 + hL)p_n.$$

The solution is easily seen to be

$$p_{n+1} = (1 + hL)^{n+1} p_0$$

for any p_0. Now, if $q_n = p_n + \lambda$, then

$$\begin{aligned} q_{n+1} &= p_{n+1} + \lambda = (1 + hL)p_n + \lambda \\ &= (1 + hL)q_n - (1 + hL)\lambda + \lambda \\ &= (1 + hL)q_n + Ah^{p+1}. \end{aligned}$$

That is, the q_n solve (3.2–13). The initial condition requires that

$$e_0 = p_0 + \lambda \qquad \text{or} \qquad p_0 = e_0 - \lambda.$$

Finally,

$$e_n \leq q_n = (1 + hL)^n e_0 + \frac{A}{L} h^p[(1 + hL)^n - 1]. \tag{3.2–14}$$

The right-hand side of the above still depends on n. The following lemma fixes this.

Lemma 3.3. $(1 + hL)^n < e^{L(b-a)}$, where $h = (b - a)/N$.

Proof. Since $n \leq N$, and $hL > 0$,

$$(1 + hL)^n < (1 + hL)^N = \left(1 + \frac{L(b - a)}{N}\right)^N.$$

Let $u = L(b - a)$. Now, by the binomial theorem

$$\left(1 + \frac{u}{N}\right)^N = \sum_{j=0}^{N} \binom{N}{j} \left(\frac{u}{N}\right)^j ,$$

where

$$\binom{N}{j} = \frac{N!}{(N-j)!\,j!} .$$

But

$$\frac{1}{N^j}\binom{N}{j} = \frac{1}{j!}\,\frac{N!}{(N-j)!\,N^j}$$

$$= \frac{1}{j!}\,\frac{N(N-1)\cdots(N-j+1)}{N\cdot N\cdots N} < \frac{1}{j!} ,$$

so that

$$\left(1 + \frac{u}{N}\right)^N < \sum_{j=0}^{N} \frac{1}{j!} u^i < e^u ,$$

with the last inequality following from Taylor's theorem.

We now have the bound

$$|Y_n - y_n| \leq e^{L(b-a)} e_0 + \frac{A}{L} h^p[e^{L(b-a)} - 1] . \tag{3.2–15}$$

Since we have assumed that $e_0 = |y_0 - Y_0| = 0$, we have

$$\max_{0 \leq n \leq N} |Y_n - y_n| \leq Ch^p$$

for some constant C, which is the desired result.

In practice one can satisfy neither the initial condition nor the single step equation exactly. Instead we have

$$Y_{n+1} = Y_n + h\Phi(x_n, Y_n) + r_n ,$$

where r_n is an error made in evaluating Y_{n+1}. If we assume that $|r_n| < r$, then (3.2–15) becomes

$$|Y_n - y_n| \leq e^{L(b-a)} e_0 + \left(\frac{A}{L} h^p + \frac{r}{Lh}\right)[e^{L(b-a)} - 1] . \tag{3.2–16}$$

If estimates were available for A and r, h could be chosen so as to minimize

$$Ah^p + \frac{r}{h} .$$

Equation (3.2–16) indicates there is not much point in taking h smaller. Of course, we have only produced an upper bound for the error. The actual error might behave quite differently.

The preceding result on convergence of single step methods, although important in itself, does not cover many interesting problems, for it was only derived for a single differential equation of first order. However, with a little more effort we can establish the convergence of single step methods for systems of first order equations, and thereby most equations of higher order. For example, the second order initial value problem

$$u'' = f(x, y, y') , \qquad u(a) = u_0 , \qquad u'(a) = u'_0 ,$$

can be transformed into a system of first order equations by introducing the variable

$$v = u' .$$

We then have

$$v' = f(x, u, v) , \qquad u' = v ,$$

with initial conditions

$$u(a) = u_0 , \qquad v(a) = u'_0 .$$

Given an equation of order m,

$$\frac{d^m u}{dx^m} = f\left(x, u, u', \ldots, \frac{d^{m-1}u}{dx^{m-1}}\right),$$

we let

$$\begin{aligned} u^1 &= u , \\ u^2 &= u' , \\ &\vdots \\ u^m &= \frac{d^{m-1}u}{dx^{m-1}} , \end{aligned}$$

to obtain the system

$$\begin{aligned} \frac{du^m}{dx} &= f(x, u^1, u^2, \ldots, u^m) , \\ \frac{du^{m-1}}{dx} &= u^m , \\ &\vdots \\ \frac{du'}{dx} &= u^2 . \end{aligned}$$

It therefore behooves us to consider arbitrary systems of the form

$$\frac{du^i}{dx} = f^i(x, u^1, \ldots, u^m) \tag{3.2–17}$$

for $i = 1, 2, \ldots, m$, with initial conditions

$$u^i(a) = u_0^i .$$

Here we have m unknown functions $u^1(x), \ldots, u^m(x)$, and m right-hand sides $f^1, \ldots, f^m$.

It is somewhat remarkable that merely by introducing some notational simplification we can analyze systems of equations in almost the same way as we did single equations. First, let u stand for the entire m-tuple or vector $(u^1, \ldots, u^m)$, that is,

$$u = (u^1, \ldots, u^m) .$$

Then (3.2–17) becomes

$$\frac{du^i}{dx} = f^i(x, u) , \qquad i = 1, 2, \ldots, m . \tag{3.2–18}$$

If we introduce the vector $f = (f^1, \ldots, f^m)$ then we might just as well write

$$\frac{du}{dx} = f(x, u) \tag{3.2–19}$$

as a shorthand symbolism for (3.2–18).

Our system now looks like a single equation and in just about every respect can be treated like one. We first have to define a linear combination of any two vectors u and v, which we take to be

$$\alpha u + \beta v = (\alpha u^1 + \beta v^1, \ldots, \alpha u^m + \beta v^m) .$$

We also need the absolute value of a vector. There are several standard ways to define this, but the most convenient for us is

$$|u| = \max_{1 \le i \le m} |u^i| .$$

We leave it to the reader to verify that

$$|\alpha u + \beta v| \le |\alpha|\,|u| + |\beta|\,|v| .$$

The single step methods are now formulated precisely as they were for one equation, and the convergence proof proceeds exactly as it did before, the reason being that once absolute values are taken to get (3.2–10) we are dealing with numbers rather than vectors. The only point that needs to be checked in detail is the fact that Heun's method is of order two. This is left for an exercise at the end of the chapter.

The algorithm for integrating the system

$$\frac{du^i}{dx} = f^i(x, u) , \qquad i = 1(1)m , \qquad u^i(0) = u_0^i$$

from $x = a$ to $x = b$ is quite simple if one has a functional evaluator, that is, a means for evaluating $f^i(x, u)$ for *any* arguments x and u. The algorithm is given below.

$$x = a\,, \qquad h = (b - a)/N\,.$$

For $i = 1(1)m$

  $U_0^i = u_0^i\,.$

For $n = 0(1)N - 1$

  For $i = 1(1)m$

    $r_i = U_n^1 + hf^i(x, U_n^1, \ldots, U_n^m)\,;$

  For $i = 1(1)m$

    $U_{n+1}^i = \dfrac{U_n^i + r_i}{2} + \dfrac{h}{2} f^i(x_n + h, r_1, \ldots, r_m)$

  $x = x + h\,.$

A major advantage of single step methods is that at any given point x one can start with a new step size. This raises a difficult practical question: What is the best value of h? The answer to this depends on the accuracy which is needed, so to determine the best h one needs a reasonably good estimate of the error made at each x. The estimates we have obtained in this section are not suitable, since they depend on the unknown exact solution. We are unable to go into the problem in this book and must therefore refer the reader to Henrici (1962a).

3.3 RICHARDSON EXTRAPOLATION

One of the results of the preceding section was that the error in Euler's method is $O(h)$, that is,

$$|y_n - Y_n| \leq Ch\,.$$

We shall show below that a sharper estimate can be obtained, namely, that

$$y_n = Y_n + e(x_n)h + O(h^2)\,, \tag{3.3–1}$$

where $e(x)$ *is a function which does not depend on* h. When such an expansion exists a method known as Richardson extrapolation can be used to improve Y_n in the sense that a new approximation $\bar{Y}_n$ is produced such that $|y_n - \bar{Y}_n| \leq C_1 h^2$. This is done as follows: Let $Y_n(h)$ be the result of doing Euler's method in steps of length h, and let $Y_n(h/2)$ correspond to steps of length $h/2$. Then by (3.3–1),

$$y_n = Y_n(h) + e(x_n)h + O(h^2)\,,$$

and also

$$y_n = Y_n\left(\frac{h}{2}\right) + e(x_n)\,\frac{h}{2} + O(h^2)\,.$$

If we eliminate $e(x_n)$ from these equations we find that

$$y_n = 2Y_n\left(\frac{h}{2}\right) - Y_n(h) + O(h^2)\,.$$

Therefore the new approximation is

$$\bar{Y}_n = 2Y_n\left(\frac{h}{2}\right) - Y_n(h) \tag{3.3–2}$$

with an error of order h^2.

To establish (3.3–1) we note that the solution of the equation $y' = f(x, y)$ satisfies the relation

$$y_{n+1} = y_n + hf(x_n, y_n) + \frac{1}{2}\,h^2 y_n'' + \frac{h^3}{3!}\,y^{(3)}(\xi)$$

by Taylor's Theorem. If we subtract (3.2–4) and let $e_n = y_n - Y_n$ (not $|y_n - Y_n|$), then

$$\begin{aligned} e_{n+1} = e_n &+ h[f(x_n, y_n) - f(x_n, y_n - e_n)] \\ &+ \frac{1}{2}\,h^2 y_n'' + \frac{h^3}{3!}\,y^{(3)}(\xi)\,. \end{aligned} \tag{3.3–3}$$

Now,

$$f(x_n, y_n - e_n) = f(x_n, y_n) - \frac{\partial f(x_n, y_n)}{\partial y}\,e_n + \frac{\partial^2 f(x_n, y^*)}{\partial y^2}\,e_n^2\,,$$

where y^* is in $[y_n, y_n - e_n]$. Substituting the above expression for $f(x_n, y_n - e_n)$ into (3.3–3) and letting $\bar{e}_n = e_n/h$, we have

$$\begin{aligned} \bar{e}_{n+1} = \bar{e}_n &+ h\,\frac{\partial f(x_n, y_n)}{\partial y}\,\bar{e}_n + h^2\,\frac{\partial^2 f}{\partial y^2}\,(\bar{e}_n)^2 \\ &+ \frac{1}{2}\,hy_n'' + \frac{h^2}{3!}\,y^{(3)}(\xi)\,. \end{aligned} \tag{3.3–4}$$

Let

$$g(x, \bar{e}) = \frac{\partial f\big(x, y(x)\big)}{\partial y}\,\bar{e} + \frac{1}{2}\,y''(x)$$

and

$$r_n = \frac{\partial^2 f(x_n, y^*)}{\partial y^2}\,(\bar{e}_n)^2 + \frac{1}{3!}\,y^{(3)}(\xi)\,,$$

so that (3.3–4) becomes

$$\bar{e}_{n+1} = \bar{e}_n + hg(x_n, \bar{e}_n) + h^2 r_n \,. \tag{3.3–5}$$

Since $|\bar{e}_n| \leq C$, there is a constant R such that

$$|r_n| \leq R \,.$$

But then (3.3–5) is nothing more than Euler's method for the equation

$$e'(x) = g\big(x, e(x)\big)\,, \qquad e(0) = 0$$

with an error $h^2 r_n$ at each step. But if $f(x, y)$ is smooth enough this differential equation has a solution $e(x)$. By (3.2–16)

$$|e(x_n) - \bar{e}_n| \leq C''h\,,$$

or

$$\bar{e}_n = e(x_n) + O(h)\,,$$

or

$$y_n = Y_n + he(x_n) + O(h^2)$$

as was to be demonstrated.

There are other contexts in which Richardson extrapolation can be used.

Whenever one has an approximation process whose error can be expanded in powers of h, then the lowest power of h can be eliminated. For example, consider the trapezoidal rule applied to a function $f(x)$ on an interval $[a, b]$. It is known that under certain circumstances [see Ralston (1965) for example],

$$\int_a^b f(x)\,dx = [\text{trapezoidal rule with interval } h] + \sum_{j=1}^{\infty} a_j h^{2j}\,.$$

Now, let $T_{0,k}$ be the result of the trapezoidal rule with 2^k subintervals. Then

$$\int_a^b f(x)\,dx = \frac{1}{3}\,(4T_{0,k+1} - T_{0,k}) + \sum_{j=2}^{\infty} b_j \left(\frac{b-a}{2^k}\right)^{2j}, \tag{3.3–6}$$

where the b_j are easily computed. Let

$$T_{1,k} = \tfrac{1}{3}(4T_{0,k+1} - T_{0,k})\,,$$

then (3.3–6) says that $T_{1,k}$ approximates $\int_a^b f(x)\,dx$ with an error having an expansion in powers of $h = (b - a)/2^k$ starting with h^4. This process can be continued to obtain error expansions starting with h^6, h^8, etc. Indeed, if we let

$$T_{m,k} = \frac{1}{4^m - 1}(4^m T_{m-1,k+1} - T_{m-1,k}), \tag{3.3-7}$$

then

$$\int_a^b f(x)\,dx = T_{m,k} + c\left(\frac{b-a}{2^k}\right)^{2(m+1)} + \cdots$$

A numerical integration procedure known as Romberg quadrature uses the above ideas in the following way. Fix m and compute $T_{0,0}$, $T_{0,1}, \ldots, T_{0,m}$. Then using (3.3-7) find $T_{1,0}, T_{1,1} \ldots, T_{1,m-1}$. Continue in this way, building up the following triangular array:

$$\begin{array}{lll} T_{0,0} & & \\ T_{0,1} & T_{1,0} & \\ \vdots & \vdots & \ddots \\ T_{0,m} & T_{1,m-1} & T_{m,0}\,. \end{array}$$

The final entry $T_{m,0}$ is the approximation to the integral. It remains to be shown that $T_{m,0}$ converges to the integral as $m \to \infty$, but this is done in Ralston (1965).

The cost of a numerical integration is usually measured by counting the number of times $f(x)$ must be computed. One of the arguments for using Romberg quadrature is that the presumably more accurate $T_{m,0}$ is obtained at the same expense as $T_{0,m}$.

3.4 THE PADÉ TABLE

One of the basic problems of numerical analysis is the efficient evaluation of special functions such as e^x, $\sin x$, etc. Since computing machines deal only with the elementary arithmetic operations it is necessary to replace the special transcendental functions by rational functions. We will suppose below that we are interested in obtaining a rational approximation to some function $f(x)$, for small x. We shall seek rational approximations of the form

$$R_{n,m}(x) = \frac{P_n(x)}{Q_m(x)}, \tag{3.4-1}$$

where

$$P_n(x) = \sum_{j=0}^{n} a_j x^j, \qquad Q_m(x) = \sum_{j=0}^{m} b_j x^j, \qquad \text{with } b_0 = 1.$$

The function $R_{n,m}(x)$ has $n + m + 1$ constants in it. The Padé table is a particular array of functions $R_{n,m}$ defined by the requirement

$$f(0) - R_{n,m}(0) = 0 \, ,$$

$$\frac{d^\alpha}{dx^\alpha} [f(x) - R_{n,m}(x)]_{x=0} = 0 \, , \qquad \alpha = 1, 2, \ldots, n + m \, .$$

Since

$$f(x) - R_{n,m}(x) = \frac{f(x)Q_m(x) - P_n(x)}{1 + \sum_{j=1}^{m} b_j x^j} \, , \tag{3.4–2}$$

the conditions at the origin will be satisfied if the coefficients of x^k for $k \leq n + m$ are zero in the numerator of (3.4–2). Setting

$$c_j = \frac{f^{(j)}(0)}{j!} \qquad \text{and} \qquad N = n + m \, ,$$

we have

$$f(x) = \sum_{j=0}^{N} c_j x^j + O(x^{N+1}) \, .$$

Then

$$\begin{aligned} f(x)Q_m(x) &= \left(\sum_{j=0}^{N} c_j x^j\right)\left(\sum_{j=0}^{m} b_j x^j\right) + O(x^{N+1}) \\ &= c_0 b_0 + (c_0 b_1 + c_1 b_0)x + \cdots \\ &\quad + \left(\sum_{r=0}^{N} b_r c_{N-r}\right) x^N + O(x^{N+1}) \, . \end{aligned}$$

We have taken $b_j = 0$ for $j > m$. The conditions become

$$\begin{aligned} &\sum_{r=0}^{j} b_r c_{j-r} = a_j \, , \qquad j \leq n \, , \\ &\sum_{r=0}^{j} b_r c_{j-r} = 0 \, , \qquad n < j \leq N \, . \end{aligned} \tag{3.4–3}$$

The solution, *if it exists*, of the inhomogeneous (because $b_0 = 1$) system (3.4–3) gives the array $R_{m,n}$.

Ralston (1965) notes that the diagonal elements $R_{n,n}(x)$ provide the best approximations for sufficiently small x. The Padé table has been computed for various functions. For example, if $f(x) = e^x$,

$$R_{2,2}(x) = \frac{12 + 6x + x^2}{12 - 6x + x^2} \, .$$

Note also that $R_{n,0}(x)$ is just the Taylor expansion.

EXERCISES

Section 3.1

1. Assume the conditions of Theorem 3.2. Let β be as defined in the proof of Theorem 3.2. Let ξ_k be any sequence in $[x_0 - \beta, x_0 + \beta]$. Show that the iteration

$$x_{k+1} = x_k - \frac{f(x_k)}{f'(\xi_k)}$$

converges to α, where $f(\alpha) = 0$. [*Hint:* Lemma 3.1 is the key.]

2. State and prove a theorem analogous to Theorem 3.2 for the iteration

$$x_{k+1} = x_k - \frac{f(x_k)}{\dfrac{f(x_k) - f(x_{k-1})}{x_k - x_{k-1}}}.$$

Note that both x_0 and x_1 have to be specified in advance. This iteration is called the method of false position or regula falsi.

Section 3.2

3. Prove that Heun's method is second order for systems.
4. Suppose the exact solution of (3.2–1), (3.2–2) satisfies $|y(x)| < A$ for $a \leq x \leq b$. Show that $|Y_n| < A$ for all n if h is sufficiently small. The significance of this is that (3.2–11) need be assumed valid only if $|Y_n| < A$ provided it is known that $|y(x)| < A$.

Section 3.3

5. (Optional) Show that Richardson extrapolation is a valid procedure for Heun's method.
6. Write a flow diagram and code for Romberg quadrature. Note: it is not necessary to store the entire triangular array. Perform the same integrations as in Exercise 7, Chapter 2.

Section 3.4

7. Find $R_{3,3}$ for e^x.
8. Tabulate $|e^x - R_{2,2}|$ and $|e^x - R_{4,0}|$ for 50 values of x in the interval $0 \leq x \leq 0.25$.
9. Given that some rational approximation is sufficiently accurate for $0 \leq x \leq 0.25$, how would you compute e^x for large x?

THE THEORY OF INTERPOLATION

THE THEORY OF INTERPOLATION

In Chapters 2 and 3 certain numerical procedures were developed on the foundation of Taylor's Theorem with remainder. In next three chapters we shall take a different approach to elementary numerical analysis, basing it on the theory of polynomial interpolation.

A polynomial of degree n is a function of the form

$$P(x) = a_n x^n + a_{n-1} x^{n-1} + \cdots + a_0 .$$

A zero of $P(x)$ of multiplicity m is a number c such that

$$0 = P(c) = P'(c) = \cdots = P^{(m-1)}(c) \qquad \text{and} \qquad P^{(m)}(c) \neq 0 .$$

A zero of multiplicity m is counted as m zeros.

Theorem 4.1. *Let $P(x)$ have degree n and let c be a zero of multiplicity m. Then if $P(x)$ is not identically zero, $m \leq n$ and*

$$P(x) = (x - c)^m r(x) ,$$

where the degree of $r(x)$ is $n - m$.

Proof. By Taylor's theorem, since $P^{(n+1)}(x) \equiv 0$,

$$P(x) = \sum_{k=0}^{n} P^{(k)}(c) \frac{(x - c)^k}{k!} .$$

If $m > n$, then $P(x) \equiv 0$, so $m \leq n$ and

$$P(x) = (x - c)^m \sum_{k=m}^{n} P^{(k)}(c) \frac{(x - c)^{k-m}}{k!} .$$

Therefore,

$$r(x) = \sum_{k=m}^{n} P^{(k)}(c) \frac{(x - c)^{k-m}}{k!} ,$$

which has degree $n - m$.

Theorem 4.2. *Let $P(x)$ have degree n. Then $P(x)$ has at most n zeros, unless it is identically zero.*

Proof. A constant polynomial, unless it is identically zero, has no zeros. Proceeding by induction, suppose the theorem true for polynomials of degree less than n. Let c be a zero of P of multiplicity m. Then

$$P(x) = (x - c)^m r(x) ,$$

where the degree of $r(x)$ is $n - m$. Since every zero of $P(x)$ other than c is a zero of $r(x)$ with the same multiplicity, and vice versa (see Exercise 1) and since the induction hypothesis says $r(x)$ has at most $n - m$ zeros, $P(x)$ has at most n zeros.

With the above theorems we may now proceed to develop the ideas of polynomial interpolation.

4.1 LAGRANGE INTERPOLATION

The Lagrange interpolation problem is the following: We are given certain distinct points, or nodes, $x_1, x_2, \ldots, x_n$. Corresponding to each node are values, $f_1, f_2, \ldots, f_n$. The problem is to find a polynomial $P(x)$ of degree $n - 1$ such that

$$P(x_i) = f_i , \qquad i = 1(1)n . \tag{4.1-1}$$

Note that (4.1-1) is a system of n equations in the n unknown coefficients of $P(x)$.

There are many reasons why one wants to construct interpolating polynomials. For example, if the numbers f_i are the values of some function $f(x)$, that is, $f_i = f(x_i)$, we might use $P(x)$ to approximate $f(x)$ when x is not a node. Another application is to use the integral or derivative of $P(x)$ instead of the integral or derivative of $f(x)$. These applications will be discussed in more detail in Chapters 5 and 6.

It is easy to exhibit a solution of the Lagrange interpolation problem. We note that if we could find polynomials $\delta_i(x)$ of degree $n - 1$ such that

$$\delta_i(x_j) = \begin{cases} 0 , & j \neq i \\ 1 , & j = i \end{cases} , \qquad i = 1(1)n , \tag{4.1-2}$$

then the function

$$P(x) = \sum_{j=1}^{n} f_j \delta_j(x) \tag{4.1-3}$$

is a polynomial of degree $n - 1$, and

$$P(x_i) = \sum_{j=1}^{n} f_j \delta_j(x_i) = f_i .$$

Thus, the general Lagrange problem is reduced to the special problem (4.1–2) which is easy to solve, namely

$$\delta_i(x) = \prod_{\substack{j=1 \\ j \neq i}}^{n} \frac{(x - x_j)}{(x_i - x_j)} . \tag{4.1–4}$$

The term $\delta_i(x)$ has $n - 1$ factors $(x - x_j)$, making it a polynomial of degree $n - 1$. It clearly satisfies (4.1–2).

Two simple examples of Lagrange interpolation are linear interpolation through two points x_1, x_2;

$$P(x) = f_1 \frac{x - x_2}{x_1 - x_2} + f_2 \frac{x - x_1}{x_2 - x_1} \tag{4.1–5}$$

and quadratic interpolation through three points x_1, x_2, x_3;

$$P(x) = f_1 \frac{(x - x_2)(x - x_3)}{(x_1 - x_2)(x_1 - x_3)} + f_2 \frac{(x - x_1)(x - x_3)}{(x_2 - x_1)(x_2 - x_3)} + f_3 \frac{(x - x_1)(x - x_2)}{(x_3 - x_1)(x_3 - x_2)} . \tag{4.1–6}$$

Note that for $n > 2$ it would be quite a chore to put $P(x)$ in the standard polynomial form $\sum a_i x^i$.

A second solution of the Lagrange problem can be given in the form of an algorithm. We take $P(x)$ to have the form

$$P(x) = b_0 + b_1(x - x_1) + b_2(x - x_1)(x - x_2) + \cdots + b_{n-1}(x - x_1) \cdots (x - x_{n-1}) . \tag{4.1–7}$$

Then, first

$$f_1 = P(x_1) = b_0 ,$$

next,

$$f_2 = P(x_2) = b_0 + b_1(x_2 - x_1) ,$$

so

$$\frac{f_2 - b_0}{x_2 - x_1} = b_1 ,$$

and so on:

$$\frac{f_i - b_0 - b_1(x_i - x_1) - \cdots - b_{i-2}(x_i - x_1) \cdots (x_i - x_{i-2})}{(x_i - x_1) \cdots (x_i - x_{i-1})} = b_{i-1} .$$

In other words, we successively determine $b_0, b_1, \ldots, b_{n-1}$.

Other forms of the Lagrange interpolating polynomial can be found in Hildebrand (1956). One important fact remains to be shown; namely, that the different forms for $P(x)$ all represent the same polynomial. Indeed, we have

Theorem 4.3. *For fixed* x_i, f_i, $i = 1(1)n$, *there is only one Lagrange interpolating polynomial.*

Proof. Suppose there were two, say $P(x)$ and $Q(x)$. Each has degree $n-1$. The difference $P(x) - Q(x)$ is also a polynomial of degree $n - 1$. But

$$P(x_i) - Q(x_i) = 0\,, \qquad i = 1(1)n\,.$$

By Theorem, 4. 2.

$$P(x) - Q(x) = 0\,.$$

4.2 HERMITE INTERPOLATION

Hermite interpolation is a generalization of Lagrange interpolation. We again have distinct nodes $x_1, x_2, \ldots, x_n$, but we now have given two sets of data, f_i and f'_i, $i = 1(1)n$, and we seek a polynomial $P(x)$ of degree $2n - 1$ such that

$$P(x_i) = f_i \tag{4.2-1}$$

and

$$P'(x_i) = f'_i\,, \qquad i = 1(1)n\,. \tag{4.2-2}$$

One solution of this problem can be obtained in the form

$$\begin{aligned} P(x) = {} & b_0 + b_1(x - x_1) + b_2(x - x_1)^2 + b_3(x - x_1)^2(x - x_2) \\ & + b_4(x - x_1)^2(x - x_2)^2 + \cdots \\ & + b_{2n-1}(x - x_n) \sum_{i=1}^{n-1} (x - x_i)^2\,. \end{aligned} \tag{4.2-3}$$

Then

$$\begin{aligned} f_1 &= P(x_1) = b_0\,, \\ f'_1 &= P'(x_1) = b_1\,, \\ f_2 &= P(x_2) = b_0 + b_1(x_2 - x_1) + b_2(x_2 - x_1)^2\,, \end{aligned}$$

or

$$\frac{f_2 - b_0 - b_1(x_2 - x_1)}{(x_2 - x_1)^2} = b_2\,.$$

Furthermore,

$$f'_2 = P'(x_2) = b_1 + 2b_2(x_2 - x_1) + b_3(x_2 - x_1)^2\,,$$

which can be solved for b_3, and so on.

For example, if $n = 2$ then $P(x)$ is cubic,

$$P(x) = b_0 + b_1(x - x_1) + b_2(x - x_1)^2 + b_3(x - x_1)^2(x - x_2)\,, \tag{4.2-4}$$

where now, if we set $h = x_2 - x_1$, we have

$$\begin{aligned} b_0 &= f_1\,, \\ b_1 &= f_1'\,, \\ b_2 &= h^{-2}[f_2 - f_1 - hf_1']\,, \\ b_3 &= h^{-3}[h(f_1' + f_2') - 2(f_1 + f_2)]\,. \end{aligned} \tag{4.2-5}$$

A solution to the Hermite problem in a form similar to (4.1–3) can also be found. We write

$$P(x) = \sum_{j=1}^{n} f_j h_j(x) + \sum_{j=1}^{n} f_j' g_j(x)\,. \tag{4.2-6}$$

Now, if

$$h_j(x_i) = \begin{cases} 0\,, & j \neq i\,, \\ 1\,, & j = i\,, \end{cases} \tag{4.2-7}$$

and if

$$g_j(x_i) = 0\,, \quad \text{all } j \text{ and } i \tag{4.2-8}$$

then (4.2–1) is satisfied. Since

$$P'(x) = \sum_{j=1}^{n} f_j h_j'(x) + \sum_{j=1}^{n} f_j' g_j'(x)\,,$$

if

$$h_j'(x_i) = 0\,, \quad \text{all } j \text{ and } i \tag{4.2-9}$$

and if

$$g_j'(x_i) = \begin{cases} 0\,, & j \neq i\,, \\ 1\,, & j = i\,, \end{cases} \tag{4.2-10}$$

then (4.2–2) is satisfied. Thus, if we can find polynomials $h_j(x)$ and $g_j(x)$ of degree $2n - 1$ satisfying (4.2–7, 8, 9, 10), we will have solved the Hermite problem.

Let

$$\pi(x) = (x - x_1)(x - x_2) \cdots (x - x_n)\,, \tag{4.2-11}$$

and let

$$l_i(x) = \frac{[\pi(x)]^2}{(x - x_i)^2}\,. \tag{4.2-12}$$

Now, both $l_i(x)$ and $l_i'(x)$ vanish at all nodes except x_i. In addition, $l_i(x)$ is a polynomial of degree $2n - 2$. If we put

$$h_i(x) = l_i(x)[a_i(x - x_i) + b_i]\,,$$

and determine a_i and b_i so that $h_i(x_i) = 1$, $h_i'(x_i) = 0$, we will have the functions $h_i(x)$. We find easily that

$$h_i(x) = \frac{l_i(x)}{l_i(x_i)}\left[1 - (x - x_i)\frac{l_i'(x_i)}{l_i(x_i)}\right],$$

or, noting that

$$\frac{l_i(x)}{l_i(x_i)} = [\delta_i(x)]^2\,,$$

where $\delta_i(x)$ is given by (4.1–4), we have

$$h_i(x) = [\delta_1(x)]^2[1 - 2(x - x_i)\delta_i'(x_i)]\,. \tag{4.2–13}$$

In a similar way we find

$$g_i(x) = (x - x_i)[\delta_i(x)]^2\,. \tag{4.2–14}$$

The question now arises, as it did for Lagrange interpolation, as to whether the two forms for $P(x)$ represent the same polynomial. As before, the answer is yes.

Theorem 4.4. *Given fixed nodes $x_1, x_2, \ldots, x_n$, and fixed data $f_1, f_1', \ldots, f_n, f_n'$, the solution of the Hermite interpolation problem is unique.*

Proof. If there were two solutions, $P(x)$ and $Q(x)$, then we would have

$$P(x_i) - Q(x_i) = 0\,, \qquad i = 1, \ldots, n\,,$$
$$P'(x_i) - Q'(x_i) = 0\,, \qquad i = 1, \ldots, n\,,$$

which means that the polynomial $P(x) - Q(x)$, of degree $2n - 1$ has n zeros each with multiplicity at least 2, or $2n$ zeros, which implies that $P(x) \equiv Q(x)$.

4.3 PIECEWISE POLYNOMIAL INTERPOLATION

The preceding sections dealt with global polynomial interpolation, but that type of interpolation has certain drawbacks. An explicit determination of the interpolating polynomials is tedious at best, but aside from that, handling polynomials of high degree leads to very difficult problems of round-off error. In additon there are analytical difficulties associated with global polynomial interpolation. For example, consider the function

$$f(x) = \frac{1}{1 + 25x^2}\,,$$

and let
$$f_i = f(x_i)\,,$$
where now we take the x_i to be equally spaced points in the interval $[-1, 1]$, that is,
$$x_i = -1 + h_n(i - 1)\,, \qquad i = 1, 2, \ldots, n\,,$$
where
$$h_n = \frac{2}{n - 1}\,.$$

Then if $P(x)$ is the Lagrange interpolating polynomial taking on the values f_i at the x_i, it is known that (see Fig. 4.1)
$$\lim_{n\to\infty} \max_{[-1\le x\le 1]} |f(x) - P(x)| = \infty\,.$$

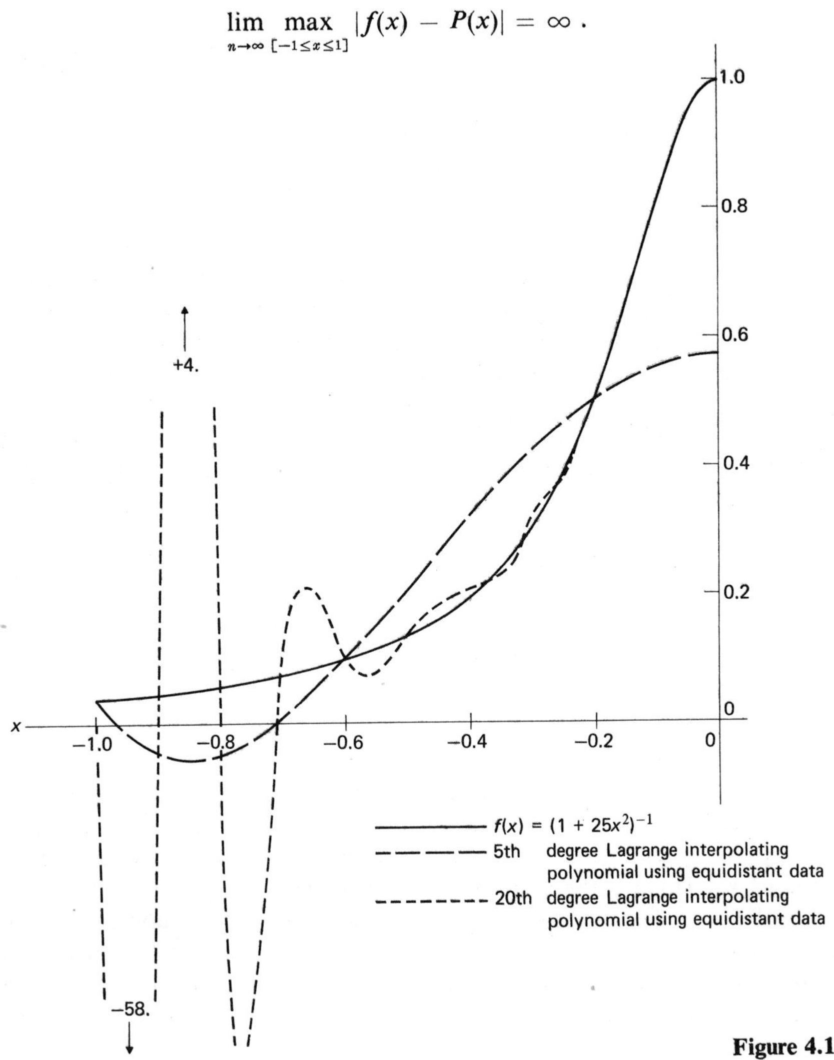

Figure 4.1

See p. 98

These difficulties can be avoided by using piecewise polynomial interpolation. The simplest example of this is piecewise linear or polygonal interpolation. Given nodes $x_1, x_2, \ldots, x_n$, and data $f_1, f_2, \ldots, f_n$, we connect pairs of points (x_i, f_i) by straight lines as in Fig. 4.2.

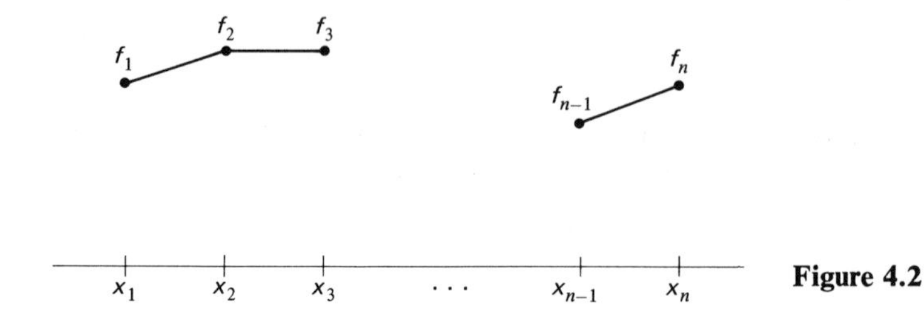

Figure 4.2

If we call the interpolating function $Q(x)$, then

$$Q(x) = f_i \frac{x - x_{i+1}}{x_i - x_{i+1}} + f_{i+1} \frac{x - x_i}{x_{i+1} - x_i}, \qquad x_i \leq x \leq x_{i+1}. \tag{4.3–1}$$

This can be generalized to piecewise quadratic interpolation, wherein one uses Lagrange interpolation of degree 2 over groups of 3 points, $[x_1, x_2, x_3]$, $[x_3, x_4, x_5]$, and so on. Clearly, one can piece together Lagrange interpolating polynomials of degree $k - 1$ over groups of k points.

Piecewise Hermite interpolation is also a possibility. In this case, given data f_i and f'_i at x_i, we form the cubic Hermite interpolating polynomial determined in the interval $[x_i, x_{i+1}]$ by the data $f_i, f'_i, f_{i+1}, f'_{i+1}$. Thus, we set

$$\begin{aligned} Q(x) = f_i + f'_i(x - x_i) &+ \frac{[f_{i+1} - f_i - (x_{i+1} - x_i)f'_i]}{(x_{i+1} - x_i)^2}(x - x_i)^2 \\ &+ \frac{(x_{i+1} - x_i)(f'_i + f'_{i+1}) - 2(f'_i + f'_{i+1})}{(x_{i+1} - x_i)^3} \\ &\times (x - x_i)^2(x - x_{i+1}) \end{aligned} \tag{4.3–2}$$

for $x_i \leq x \leq x_{i+1}$.

Still another type of piecewise polynomial interpolation exists which has many interesting aspects and applications. Let us consider the piecewise cubic $Q(x)$ in (4.3–2), and let us note that $Q(x)$ is a continuous function of x. This is certainly true if x is not a node, but even if $x = x_i$, Q is continuous, because $Q(x_i-)$, that is, the value of $Q(x_i)$ computed using the cubic in $[x_{i-1}, x_i]$, is the same as $Q(x_i+)$, the value of $Q(x_i)$ using the cubic in $[x_i, x_{i+1}]$, both values being equal to f_i. It is also true that $Q'(x)$ is continuous, for $Q'(x_i-) = Q'(x_i+) = f'_i$. However, it is *not* in general true that $Q''(x)$ is continuous at x_i. Therefore, one might well ask if it is possible to have a smoother piecewise cubic, that is, one with continuous first *and* second derivatives. Such a function is called a cubic spline. Let us see how to construct an interpolating spline, that is, a spline taking on the values f_i at the nodes x_i.

Let $s(x)$ be the desired spline. Since it is to have a continuous second derivative, $s''(x)$ is defined at $x = x_i$. So, let

$$s_i'' = s''(x_i) .$$

Now, if $s(x)$ is cubic in $[x_i, x_{i+1}]$, then $s''(x)$ is linear in that interval, so we may write

$$s''(x) = s_i'' + \frac{(x - x_i)}{x_{i+1} - x_i} (s_{i+1}'' - s_i'') .$$

Then

$$\begin{aligned} s'(x) &= s_i' + \int_{x_i}^{x} s''(t)\, dt \\ &= s_i' + s_i''(x - x_i) + \frac{s_{i+1}'' - s_i''}{(x_{i+1} - x_i)} \frac{(x - x_i)^2}{2} \end{aligned}$$

and

$$s(x) = s(x_i) + s_i'(x - x_i) + s_i'' \frac{(x - x_i)^2}{2} + \frac{s_{i+1}'' - s_i''}{(x_{i+1} - x_i)} \frac{(x - x_i)^3}{6} . \tag{4.3-3}$$

The constants $s(x_i)$ and s_i' can be eliminated by using the conditions

$$s(x_i) = f_i , \qquad \text{and} \qquad s(x_{i+1}) = f_{i+1} ,$$

which give

$$s_i' = (x_{i+1} - x_i)^{-1}\left(f_{i+1} - f_i - s_i'' \frac{(x_{i+1} - x_i)^2}{2} - \frac{s_{i+1}'' - s_i''}{6} (x_{i+1} - x_i)^2\right) . \tag{4.3-4}$$

At this point the spline $s(x)$ is written in terms of the unknown second derivatives s_i''. These can be eliminated by applying the condition that the first derivative be continuous at x_i. For convenience let us suppose we have equal intervals

$$x_{i+1} - x_i = h .$$

Then from (4.3-3)

$$s'(x_i) = s_i' .$$

However, for $x_{i-1} \leq x \leq x_i$ we have

$$s(x) = s(x_{i-1}) + s'_{i-1}(x - x_{i-1}) + s''_{i-1}\frac{(x - x_{i-1})^2}{2} + \frac{s''_i - s''_{i-1}}{h}\frac{(x - x_{i-1})^3}{6}$$

and

$$s'(x_i) = s'_{i-1} + \frac{h}{2}(s''_i + s''_{i-1}) .$$

If we equate the two expressions for $s'(x_i)$ and use (4.3–4), we find that

$$s''_{i-1} + 4s''_i + s''_{i+1} = \frac{6}{h^2}(f_{i+1} - 2f_i + f_{i-1}) \tag{4.3–5}$$

for $i = 2, 3, \ldots, n - 1$.

The system (4.3–5) contains only $n - 2$ equations, but there are n unknown s''_i. We therefore impose two additional conditions, which we take to be

$$s''_1 = s''_n = 0 . \tag{4.3–6}$$

The system can now be solved by elmination. Since $s''_1 = 0$, the first equation can be solved for s''_2 as a function of s''_3. The next equation is

$$s''_2 + 4s''_3 + s''_4 = \frac{6}{h^2}(f_4 - 2f_3 + f_2) .$$

If we replace s''_2 by its expression in terms of s''_3, we can next solve for s''_3 as a function of s''_4. We continue in this way until we obtain s''_{n-1} as a function of s''_n. Since the latter is zero, we can obtain s''_{n-1}, then s''_{n-2}, and so on. This can be put in algorithmic form as follows: Let

$$s''_{i-1} = p_{i-1}s''_i + q_{i-1} . \tag{4.3–7}$$

If we take $p_1 = q_1 = 0$, then $s''_1 = 0$. Replace s''_{i-1} in (4.3–5) by the right side of (4.3–7), obtaining

$$s''_i = \frac{-1}{4 + p_{i-1}} s''_{i+1} + \frac{(6/h^2)(f_{i+1} - 2f_i + f_{i-1}) - q_{i-1}}{4 + p_{i-1}} .$$

This has the same form as (4.3–7), therefore

$$\begin{aligned} p_i &= \frac{-1}{4 + p_{i-1}} , \\ q_i &= \frac{(6/h^2)(f_{i+1} - 2f_i + f_{i-1}) - q_{i-1}}{4 + p_{i-1}} . \end{aligned} \tag{4.3–8}$$

Note that if $|p_{i-1}| \leq 1$, then

$$|p_i| \leq \frac{1}{|4 + p_{i-1}|} \leq \frac{1}{4 - |p_{i-1}|} \leq \frac{1}{3}\,.$$

Thus, every p_i satisfies $|p_i| \leq 1$ (since $p_1 = 0$) and none of the denominators in (4.3–8) vanish. The final algorithm is

$$p_1 = q_1 = 0$$

For $i = 2(1)(n-1)$

$$p_i = \frac{-1}{4 + p_{i-1}}$$

$$q_i = \frac{(6/h^2)(f_{i+1} - 2f_i + f_{i-1}) - q_{i-1}}{4 + p_{i-1}}$$

$$s_n'' = 0$$

For $i = 1(1)(n-1)$

$$s_{n-i}'' = p_{n-i}s_{n-i+1}'' + q_{n-i}\,.$$

Once all the s_i'' have been calculated, the spline can be computed from (4.3–3) and (4.3–4).

With the aid of the above algorithm we can easily show that there is only one interpolating spline for the fixed nodes x_i and the fixed data f_i. If there were two, say $s(x)$ and $\bar{s}(x)$, then their difference $u(x) = s(x) - \bar{s}(x)$ would be a spline which vanished at each node. We would then have

$$u_{i-1}'' + 4u_i'' + u_{i+1}'' = 0\,, \qquad i = 2, 3, \ldots, n-1$$

and

$$u_1'' = u_n'' = 0\,.$$

Now consider the algorithm, which starts off with $p_1 = q_1 = 0$, so that

$$p_2 = -\tfrac{1}{4}\,, \qquad q_2 = 0\,;$$

that is,

$$4u_2'' + u_3'' = 0\,,$$

which is certainly true. It follows by induction that all the q_i are zero, or

$$u_{i-1}'' = p_{i-1}u_i''\,.$$

Since $u_n'' = 0$, all the u_i'' are zero, and therefore $u''(x) \equiv 0$. Thus $u(x)$ is linear and vanishes at x_1 and x_n, so

$$0 \equiv u(x) = s(x) - \bar{s}(x)\,.$$

4.4 THE ERROR OF INTERPOLATION

Suppose the data f_i corresponding to the nodes x_i are the values of some function $f(x)$:

$$f_i = f(x_i)\,, \qquad i = 1(1)n\,.$$

Let $x_1 < x_2 < \cdots < x_n$.

The various interpolating functions constructed in the first three sections of this chapter have the property that they agree with $f(x)$ at the nodes. What we will investigate in this section is how much the interpolating functions differ from $f(x)$ when x is not a node.

Consider first Lagrange interpolation, with $P(x)$ given by (4.1–3). The error $f(x) - P(x)$ vanishes at the x_i. We can separate this behavior out by writing

$$f(x) = P(x) + \pi(x)G(x)\,, \tag{4.4–1}$$

where

$$\pi(x) = \prod_{i=1}^{n} (x - x_i) \tag{4.4–2}$$

and $G(x)$ is to be determined.

Now, $G(x)$ is continuous at any x which is not a node. However, by L'Hospital's rule

$$G(x_i) = \lim_{x \to x_i} \frac{f'(x) - P'(x)}{\pi'(x)} = \frac{f'(x_i) - P'(x_i)}{\pi'(x_i)}\,. \tag{4.4–3}$$

Since $\pi'(x_i) \neq 0$, $G(x)$ is also continuous at any node x_i.

Let x be fixed and consider the following function of z,

$$H(z) = f(z) - P(z) - \pi(z)G(x)\,.$$

Since $f(x_i) = P(x_i)$, and $\pi(x_i) = 0$, it follows that

$$H(x_i) = 0\,, \qquad i = 1(1)n\,.$$

But also, $H(x) = 0$, by (4.4–1). Suppose $x \neq x_i$. Then $H(z)$ vanishes at $n + 1$ distinct points. By Rolle's theorem $H'(z)$ vanishes at some point strictly between each adjacent pair of those points, so $H'(z)$ vanishes at n distinct points. Similarly $H''(z)$ vanishes at $n - 1$ distincts points, and so on, until we see that there is a point ξ, *depending on* x, such that

$$H^{(n)}(\xi) = 0\,.$$

But, because $P(z)$ is a polynomial of degree $n - 1$,

$$\begin{aligned} 0 = H^{(n)}(\xi) &= f^{(n)}(\xi) - \pi^{(n)}(\xi)G(x) \\ &= f^{(n)}(\xi) - n!\, G(x) \end{aligned}$$

or

$$G(x) = \frac{f^{(n)}(\xi)}{n!}. \tag{4.4-4}$$

This was derived under the assumption that $x \neq x_i$. If x is some node x_i then $H(z)$ only vanishes at n distinct points. But,

$$H'(z) = f'(z) - P'(z) - \pi'(z)G(x_i),$$

so, by (4.4-3)

$$H'(x_i) = 0,$$

and so we may still conclude that $H'(z)$ vanishes at n distinct points, and (4.4-4) still holds.

If a bound for $f^{(n)}(x)$ were known, then

$$|f(x) - P(x)| \leq \frac{\max_x |\pi(x)|}{n!} \max_\xi |f^n(\xi)|. \tag{4.4-5}$$

A result similar to (4.4-4) can be obtained for Hermite interpolation. We now set

$$q(x) = \pi^2(x),$$

and

$$f(x) = P(x) + q(x)G(x),$$

where $P(x)$ is given by (4.2-6). Since $q'(x_i) = 0$, but $q''(x_i) \neq 0$, we have that $G(x)$ is continuous and

$$G(x_i) = \frac{f''(x_i) - p''(x_i)}{q''(x_i)}.$$

Again we define

$$H(z) = f(z) - P(z) - q(z)G(x). \tag{4.4-6}$$

Suppose $x \neq x_i$. Then H vanishes at all the x_i and at x. As before, H' vanishes at n distinct points, none of which are any x_i. But $H'(x_i) = 0$, from (4.4-6), so H' vanishes at $2n$ distinct points. Then H'' vanishes at $2n - 1$ distinct points, and so on, until we see that there is a ξ such that

$$H^{(2n)}(\xi) = 0,$$

or, since $P(z)$ is a polynomial of degree $2n - 1$,

$$G(x) = \frac{1}{(2n)!} f^{(2n)}(\xi). \tag{4.4-7}$$

If $x = x_i$, then $H''(x_i) = 0$, and (4.4–7) still holds. There is another way to represent the error of interpolation which has greater applicability than the above. We first need to note that interpolation is a *linear process*, in the following sense. For any function $f(x)$, let P_f be one of the interpolating functions (Lagrange, Hermite, or spline) using a fixed set of nodes. Then for any two functions f and g

$$P_{\alpha f+\beta g} = \alpha P_f + \beta P_g . \tag{4.4–8}$$

For Lagrange interpolation this follows immediately from (4.1–3), for

$$P_{\alpha f+\beta g} = \sum_{j=1}^{n} (\alpha f_j + \beta g_j)\delta_j(x) = \alpha P_f + \beta P_g .$$

For Hermite interpolation it follows in the same way from (4.2–6). For spline interpolation we proceed as follows: Let

$$\delta_{ij} = \begin{cases} 1 & \text{if } i = j , \\ 0 & \text{if } i \neq j . \end{cases}$$

Let $\phi_i(x)$ be the unique spline satisfying

$$\phi_i(x_j) = \delta_{ij} .$$

Then if

$$P_f = \sum_{i=1}^{n} f_i \phi_i(x) ,$$

then P_f is the interpolating spline to $f(x)$. The linearity now follows.

Now, let P be any interpolation process which is linear in the sense of (4.4–8), and which is exact for polynomials of degree m, that is, if $q(x)$ is a polynomial of degree m,

$$P_q = q .$$

For a given function $f(x)$, from Taylor's theorem we have

$$f(x) = f(x_1) + f'(x_1)(x - x_1) + \cdots + f^{(m)}(x_1)\frac{(x - x_1)^m}{m!} + \int_{x_1}^{x} f^{(m+1)}(t)\frac{(x - t)^m}{m!}\,dt .$$

Introduce the function

$$K(x, t) = \begin{cases} \dfrac{(x - t)^m}{m!} , & x_1 \leq t < x , \\ 0 , & x \leq t \leq x_n , \end{cases}$$

so that

$$f(x) = \sum_{j=0}^{m} f^{(j)}(x_1)\frac{(x - x_1)^j}{j!} + \int_{x_1}^{x_n} K(x, t) f^{(m+1)}(t)\, dt$$
$$= F(x) + \bar{F}(x)\,,$$

where

$$F(x) = \sum_{j=0}^{m} f^{(j)}(x_1)\frac{(x - x_1)^j}{j!}\,,$$
$$\bar{F}(x) = \int_{x_1}^{x_n} K(x, t) f^{(m+1)}(t)\, dt\,.$$

Then

$$P_f = P_F + P_{\bar{F}} = F + P_{\bar{F}} \qquad \text{or} \qquad f - P_f = \bar{F} - P_{\bar{F}}\,.$$

Obviously,

$$P_{\bar{F}} = \int_{x_1}^{x_n} P_{K(\cdot,t)} f^{(m+1)}(t)\, dt\,, \tag{4.4–9}$$

where $P_{K(\cdot,t)}$ is the interpolating function for $K(x, t)$ considered as a function of x. Thus

$$f(x) - P_f(x) = \int_{x_1}^{x_n} [K(x, t) - P_{K(\cdot,t)}] f^{(m+1)}(t)\, dt\,. \tag{4.4–10}$$

The upshot of this is that it is only necessary to find the error of interpolation for the function $K(x, t)$ in order to represent the error for any function. This is a special case of the Peano Kernel theorem. See P. J. Davis (1965).

As an application, consider linear interpolation through two points. This is exact for linear polynomials, so $m = 1$, and

$$K(x,t) = \begin{cases} x - t\,, & x_1 \le t < x\,, \\ 0\,, & x \le t \le x_2\,, \end{cases}$$

$$P_{K(\cdot,t)} = K(x_1, t)\frac{x - x_2}{x_1 - x_2} + K(x_2, t)\frac{x - x_1}{x_2 - x_1}$$
$$= (x_2 - t)\frac{(x - x_1)}{x_2 - x_1}\,.$$

Then for $x_1 \le t < x$

$$K(x, t) - P_{K(\cdot,t)} = x - t - (x_2 - t)\frac{(x - x_1)}{x_2 - x_1} = \frac{(t - x_1)(x - x_2)}{x_2 - x_1}\,,$$

and for $x \le t \le x_2$

$$K(x, t) - P_{K(\cdot,t)} = \frac{(x_2 - t)(x - x_1)}{x_2 - x_1}\,.$$

So, in this case, if we put

$$G(x, t) = \begin{cases} \dfrac{(t - x_1)(x - x_2)}{x_2 - x_1}, & x_1 \le t < x, \\ \dfrac{(x_2 - t)(x - x_1)}{x_2 - x_1}, & x \le t \le x_2, \end{cases} \tag{4.4-11}$$

then for $x_1 \le x \le x_2$,

$$f(x) - P_f(x) = \int_{x_1}^{x_2} G(x, t) f''(t)\, dt\,. \tag{4.4-12}$$

The explicit calculation of $K(x, t) - P_{K(\bullet, t)}$ in other cases is quite difficult.

EXERCISES

Section 4.1

1. Finish the proof of Theorem 4.2.
2. Write an algorithm for evaluating the Lagrange interpolating polynomial in the form given in (4.1-7).
3. For a given function $f(x)$ and fixed nodes $x_1, x_2, \ldots, x_n$, define kth order divided difference,

$$f[x_1, x_2, \ldots, x_k, x] = \frac{f[x_1, x_2, \ldots, x_{k-1}, x] - f[x_1, x_2, \ldots, x_k]}{x - x_k}$$

for $k \ge 2$, and

$$f[x_1, x] = \frac{f(x) - f(x_1)}{x - x_1}\,.$$

Prove that $b_k = f[x_1, x_2, \ldots, x_{k+1}]$, $k \ge 1$.

Section 4.2

4. Generalized Hermite interpolation is the following: Given distinct nodes, $x_1, x_2, \ldots, x_n$ and n sets of data $f_i, f_i', f_i'', \ldots, f_i^{(m)}$, $i = 1(1)n$, find the polynomial $P(x)$ of degree $(m + 1)n - 1$ such that $P^{(l)}(x_i) = f_i^{(l)}$, $i = 1(1)n$, $l = 0(1)m$. Solve this problem by generalizing (4.2-3) and prove that $P(x)$ is unique.
5. Let $f(x) = (1 + 25x^2)^{-1}$ and let $x_i = -1 + (2/(n - 1))(i - 1)$, $i = 1(1)n$. Write a program to evaluate the Lagrange and Hermite interpolating polynomials, with $f_i = f(x_i)$, $f_i' = f'(x_i)$. Use $n = 5$ and $n = 10$. Tabulate the difference between the polynomials and $f(x)$ at 50 equally spaced points in $[-1, 1]$.

Section 4.3

6. Write a program to evaluate the interpolating spline for any given set of data f_i and any number of equally spaced nodes.

7. Set up the equations for the interpolating spline with the conditions that s_0' and s_n' are given. [*Hint:* Eliminate the second derivatives and find the system of equations satisfied by the first derivatives.]

Section 4.4

8. Find $K(x, t) - P_{K(\cdot,t)}$ explicitly for Hermite interpolation using 2 points, $x_1 < x_2$.
9. Let $K(x, t) - P_{K(\cdot,t)} = G(x, t)$, where the set of nodes is fixed, and P refers to either Lagrange or Hermite interpolation only. Now, the function $f - P_f$ satisfies certain homogeneous conditions at the nodes. For example, in the Hermite case both $f - P_f$ and $f' - P_f'$ vanish at the nodes. Let $g(t)$ be continuous on $[x_1, x_n]$. Prove that

$$e(x) = \int_{x_1}^{x_n} G(x, t)g(t)\,dt\,,$$

satisfies the same homogeneous conditions, is $m + 1$ times continuously differentiable, where $m = n - 1$ for Lagrange, $2n - 1$ for Hermite and

$$\frac{d^{m+1}}{dx^{m+1}}\,e(x) = g(x)\,, \qquad x_1 < x < x_n\,.$$

Chapter Five

APPLICATIONS OF INTERPOLATION, PART 1

APPLICATIONS OF INTERPOLATION, PART 1

The various processes of interpolation provide greater versatility in the construction of numerical integration procedures than does Taylor's theorem. We present two general classes of integration rules, and then in Section 5.3 discuss error bounds.

5.1 CONSTRUCTION OF INTEGRATION RULES

Since polynomials can be integrated in closed form, any of the interpolating polynomials or piecewise polynomial interpolating functions can be integrated. If the data f_i are the values of a particular function $f(x)$ evaluated at the nodes x_i, that is to say, $f(x_i) = f_i$, then we may think of the interpolating function as representing $f(x)$ everywhere in some interval. Accordingly, the integral of the interpolating function may be taken as an approximation to the integral of $f(x)$.

The trapezoidal rule and Simpson's rule are easily generated in this way. Putting

$$\begin{aligned} P(x) &= \frac{x - x_{i+1}}{x_i - x_{i+1}} f_i + \frac{x - x_i}{x_{i+1} - x_i} f_{i+1}, \qquad x_i \leq x \leq x_{i+1} \\ &= h^{-1}[(f_{i+1} - f_i)x + f_i x_{i+1} - f_{i+1} x_i], \qquad x_i \leq x \leq x_{i+1}, \end{aligned}$$

we have

$$\int_{x_0}^{x_n} P(x)\,dx = \sum_{i=0}^{n-1} \int_{x_i}^{x_{i+1}} P(x)\,dx = \sum \frac{h}{2}(f_{i+1} + f_i)\,.$$

Similarly, if we set

$$\begin{aligned} P(x) &= f_i \frac{(x - x_{i+1})(x - x_{i+2})}{(x_i - x_{i+1})(x_i - x_{i+2})} + f_{i+1} \frac{(x - x_i)(x - x_{i+2})}{(x_{i+1} - x_i)(x_{i+1} - x_{i+2})} \\ &\quad + f_{i+2} \frac{(x - x_i)(x - x_{i+1})}{(x_{i+2} - x_i)(x_{i+2} - x_{i+1})}, \qquad x_i \leq x \leq x_{i+2}, \end{aligned}$$

we have

$$\int_{x_0}^{x_n} P(x)\,dx = \sum_{j=0}^{(n-2)/2} \int_{x_{2j}}^{x_{2j+2}} P(x)\,dx$$

$$= \sum_{j=0}^{(n-2)/2} \frac{h}{3}\,[f_{2j} + 4f_{2j+1} + f_{2j+2}]\,.$$

In the same way we can piece together Lagrange interpolating polynomials of higher degree and then integrate. The resulting integration rules are called Newton-Cotes formulas. They have some undesirable properties and are not used very much [see Hildebrand (1956), or Ralston (1965)].

An interesting formula results if the piecewise cubic obtained by patching together Hermite interpolating polynomials is integrated. In this case from (4.2–5),

$$P(x) = f_i + f_i'(x - x_i) + (f_{i+1} - f_i - hf_i')\,\frac{(x - x_i)^2}{h^2}$$

$$+ [h(f_i' + f_{i+1}') - 2(f_i + f_{i+1})]\,\frac{(x - x_i)^2}{h^3}\,(x - x_{i+1})\,,$$

for $x_i \leq x \leq x_{i+1}$. Then

$$\int_{x_0}^{x_n} P(x)\,dx = \sum_{i=0}^{n-1} \int_{x_i}^{x_{i+1}} P(x)\,dx = \sum \Big\{hf_i + \frac{h^2}{2} f_i' + \frac{h}{3}(f_{i+1} - f_i - hf_i')$$

$$- \frac{h}{12}\,[h(f_i' + f_{i+1}') - 2(f_{i+1} - f_i)]\Big\}$$

$$= \frac{h^2}{12}\,(f_0' - f_n') + \frac{h}{2}\sum_{i=0}^{n-1} (f_{i+1} + f_i)\,.$$

All derivatives of f have dropped out except f_0', f_n'. This formula is called the trapezoidal rule with endpoint correction.

An integration rule can also be obtained from the cubic splines in several ways. One can express the integral of each cubic in terms of the unknown coefficients, then use the method of Chapter 4 to find the coefficients, thereby obtaining the integral. Another, somewhat more convenient way is to write

$$P(x) = \sum f_i \phi_i(x)\,,$$

where $\phi_i(x)$ is a spline such that

$$\phi_i(x_i) = 1\,, \qquad \phi_i(x_j) = 0\,, \qquad i \neq j\,.$$

Then

$$\int P(x)\,dx = \sum f_i \int \phi_i(x)\,dx = \sum A_i^{(n)} f_i\,, \tag{5.1–1}$$

where we have set

$$A_i^{(n)} = \int \phi_i(x)\, dx\ .$$

The superscript is to show that $A_i^{(n)}$ depends on the number of interpolation points (and on their values, of course). The $A_i^{(n)}$ could be computed once for all, for a fixed set of points, and then (5.1–1) would give the spline approximate integration for $\int f(x)\, dx$. The spline integration formula has several interesting properties which are, however, beyond the scope of this book.

5.2 GAUSSIAN QUADRATURE

In the integration formulas developed so far it has been implied that there was no choice about the points at which the integrand could be evaluated. This would be the case, for example, if the data came from experimental measurements made at prescribed times. It may happen, however, that the value of the integrand $f(x)$ can be generated by the computer for any argument x. In that case one might be led to the following question. Suppose it is required to compute $\int_0^1 f(x)\, dx$ using a formula of the form $a_1 f(x_1) + \cdots + a_n f(x_n)$. Does there exist a "best" choice for the points x_i and the coefficients a_i? As it stands, the question makes no sense without having a definition for what is meant by "best." There are many such definitions, each having an associated best quadrature formula. The one we shall pursue leads to what is known as Gaussian quadrature.

We will find an integration rule that will do the best possible job on polynomials, namely, it will integrate polynomials exactly. Furthermore, our rule will exactly integrate polynomials of as high a degree as possible. So, we fix an integer n, and look for n distinct points $x_1, \ldots, x_n$, and n coefficients $a_1, \ldots, a_n$ such that

$$\int_0^1 p(x)\, dx = \sum_{i=1}^{n} a_i p(x_i) \tag{5.2–1}$$

for *every* polynomial $p(x)$ of degree m, with m still to be determined. We can generalize this a bit by supposing there is given a fixed positive continuous weight function $w(x)$, and then we ask that

$$\int_0^1 p(x) w(x)\, dx = \sum_{i=1}^{n} a_i p(x_i)\ . \tag{5.2–2}$$

Having found the a_i and x_i, we will then use $\sum a_i f(x_i)$ as an *approximation* to $\int_0^1 f(x) w(x)\, dx$.

The first question we can easily answer is that of finding the largest possible value of m, for if we let

$$p(x) = \prod_{i=1}^{n} (x - x_i)^2 ,$$

then

$$0 = \sum a_i p(x_i) ,$$

but

$$\int_0^1 p(x)w(x)\, dx > 0 .$$

So,

$$m < 2n .$$

On the other hand, for any x_i's we can find coefficients a_i such that the integration rule is exact for polynomials of degree $n - 1$, because, if we put

$$\delta_i(x) = \prod_{j \neq i} \frac{x - x_j}{x_i - x_j} ,$$

we have for any $p(x)$ of degree $n - 1$

$$p(x) = \sum \delta_i(x) p(x_i) .$$

This follows from the uniqueness of Lagrange interpolation. Then

$$\int_0^1 p(x)w(x)\, dx = \sum \left[\int_0^1 \delta_i(x)w(x)\, dx \right] p(x_i)$$

so,

$$a_i = \int_0^1 \delta_i(x)w(x)\, dx .$$

Thus, $n - 1 \leq m < 2n$.

Once we have found the x_i's, the a_i's are determined, for we just take $p(x)$ to be $\delta_j(x)$, so that

$$a_j = \sum a_i p(x_i) = \int_0^1 p(x)w(x)\, dx = \int_0^1 \delta_j(x)w(x)\, dx$$

for $j = 1, 2, \ldots, n$. Therefore we can reformulate the problem in the following way: Let $p(x)$ be any polynomial of degree $m \geq n - 1$, and let $\bar{p}(x)$ be the Lagrange interpolating polynomial of degree $n - 1$ which agrees with $p(x)$ at the x_i. Let

$$a_i = \int_0^1 \delta_i(x)w(x)\, dx . \tag{5.2-3}$$

Since we want $\int_0^1 p(x)w(x)\,dx = \sum a_i p(x_i)$, and we know that

$$\int_0^1 \bar{p}(x)w(x)\,dx = \sum a_i \bar{p}(x_i) = \sum a_i p(x_i)\,,$$

the problem is to find $x_1, \ldots, x_n$ such that

$$\int_0^1 [p(x) - \bar{p}(x)]w(x)\,dx = 0$$

for any polynomial $p(x)$ of degree m.

We will solve this form of the problem for $m = 2n - 1$, which is the largest that m can be. To do this we will need an explicit representation for $p - \bar{p}$. This can be obtained from equation (4.1–7). First, still assuming that the x_i exist, let $y_1, \ldots, y_n$ be n distinct points which are also distinct from the x_i. Since $p(x)$ is its own Lagrange interpolating polynomial for the points $x_1, \ldots, x_n, y_1, \ldots, y_n$ we have

$$\begin{aligned} p(x) = {} & [b_0 + b_1(x - x_1) + \cdots b_{n-1}(x - x_1) \cdots (x - x_{n-1})] \\ & + \prod_{i=1}^{n} (x - x_i)[b_n + b_{n+1}(x - y_1) \\ & + \cdots b_{2n-1}(x - y_1) \cdots (x - y_{n-1})]\,. \end{aligned}$$

Since the first bracket is equal to $p(x_i)$ for $x = x_0$, we have

$$p(x) = \bar{p}(x) + \prod_{i=1}^{n} (x - x_i)R(x)\,,$$

where $R(x)$ is a polynomial of degree $n - 1$.

The Gaussian quadrature problem is then solved if we can find points $x_1, \ldots, x_n$ such that

$$\int_0^1 \prod_{i=1}^{n} (x - x_i)R(x)w(x)\,dx = 0 \tag{5.2–4}$$

for *every* polynomial $R(x)$ of degree $n - 1$. The remarkable thing is that such x_i do exist, and we shall prove this by induction. First, note that the x_i depend on n, so that we must actually find the elements of the following triangular array:

$$\begin{array}{llll} x_1^1 & & & \\ x_1^2 & x_2^2 & & \\ x_1^3 & x_2^3 & x_3^3 & \\ \vdots & & & \\ x_1^n & x_2^n & \cdots & x_n^n\,. \end{array}$$

If we let

$$p_n(x) = \prod_{i=1}^{n} (x - x_i^n) , \tag{5.2–5}$$

then for $k = 1, 2, \ldots, n$, we must find polynomials of this form such that $\int p_k(x)R_{k-1}(x)w(x)\,dx = 0$, where $R_j(x)$ is any polynomial of degree j. The following lemma furnishes a crucial simplification of this problem.

Lemma 5.1. For $k = 0, 1, \ldots, n$ let $p_k(x)$ be a polynomial of degree k such that the coefficient of x^k is 1. Then any polynomial R_n of degree n can be written uniquely as

$$R_n(x) = \sum_{j=0}^{n} a_j p_j(x) .$$

Proof. This is certainly true for $n = 0$. Suppose it is true for $k = 0, 1, \ldots, n - 1$. Then if

$$R_n(x) = \sum_{k=0}^{n} b_k x^k ,$$

we have

$$R_n(x) = b_n p_n(x) + R_{n-1}(x) .$$

By the induction hypothesis

$$R_n(x) = b_n p_n(x) + \sum_{j=0}^{n-1} a_j p_j(x) .$$

The uniqueness is obvious.

Some notation will be useful at this point. For any two functions $u(x)$, $v(x)$, let

$$(u, v) = \int_0^1 u(x)v(x)w(x)\,dx .$$

(u, v) is called the scalar product of u and v. If $(u, v) = 0$ we say u and v are orthogonal. Note that

$$(u, a_1v_1 + \cdots + a_kv_k) = \sum_{i=1}^{k} a_i(u, v_i) .$$

We also write

$$\sqrt{(u, u)} = ||u|| .$$

$||u||$ is called the norm of u.

It follows from Lemma 5.1 that it is sufficient to construct the $p_k(x)$ so that

$$(p_k, p_j) = 0 \qquad \text{for} \qquad j < k , \qquad k = 1, 2, \ldots, n$$

for then

$$(p_n, R_{n-1}) = \left(p_n, \sum_{i=0}^{n-1} a_i p_i\right) = \sum_{i=0}^{n-1} a_i (p_n, p_i) = 0 .$$

The polynomials $p_k(x)$ are called orthogonal polynomials. They are obtained inductively as follows: First, put

$$p_{-1}(x) = 0 , \qquad p_0(x) = 1$$

and suppose we have found $p_0, p_1, \ldots, p_{n-1}$ such that $(p_k, p_j) = 0, j < k$, $k \le n - 1$, and such that the leading coefficient of each p_k is 1. It follows from Lemma 5.1 that we may write

$$p_n(x) = xp_{n-1}(x) + \sum_{j=0}^{n-1} a_j p_j(x) .$$

Then

$$\begin{aligned}(p_n, p_k) &= (xp_{n-1}, p_k) + \sum_{j=0}^{n-1} a_j (p_j, p_k) \\ &= (xp_{n-1}, p_k) + a_k (p_k, p_k)\end{aligned}$$

by the induction hypothesis. But, since

$$(xp_{n-1}, p_k) = (p_{n-1}, xp_k) ,$$

then if $k \le n - 3$,

$$(xp_{n-1}, p_k) = 0 .$$

Therefore

$$(p_n, p_k) = a_k (p_k, p_k) , \qquad k \le n - 3 .$$

Since $(p_k, p_k) \ne 0$, (p_n, p_k) will vanish if and only if $a_k = 0$, $k \le n - 3$. So $p_n(x)$ has the form

$$p_n(x) = (x - a_n) p_{n-1}(x) + b_n p_{n-2}(x) .$$

The remaining two orthogonality conditions will determine a_n and b_n, namely

$$\begin{aligned}0 = (p_n, p_{n-2}) &= (xp_{n-1}, p_{n-2}) - a_n (p_{n-1}, p_{n-2}) + b_n \|p_{n-2}\|^2 \\ &= (xp_{n-1}, p_{n-2}) + b_n \|p_{n-2}\|^2 , \\ 0 = (p_n, p_{n-1}) &= (xp_{n-1}, p_{n-1}) - a_n \|p_{n-1}\|^2 .\end{aligned}$$

We note that

$$(xp_{n-1}, p_{n-2}) = \|p_{n-1}\|^2 ,$$

(proof is left as an exercise), so we may summarize as follows. The polynomials $p_k(x)$ defined by the following algorithm are orthogonal:

$$p_{-1} = 0 ,$$
$$p_0 = 1 .$$

$$\text{For } k = 1(1)n$$

(5.2–6)
$$a_k = \frac{(xp_{k-1}, p_{k-1})}{||p_{k-1}||^2}$$
$$b_k = -\frac{||p_{k-1}||^2}{||p_{k-2}||^2}$$
$$p_k(x) = (x - a_k)p_{k-1}(x) + b_k p_{k-2}(x) .$$

The nice thing about this algorithm is that only two integrations have to be done at each step, namely (p_{k-1}, p_{k-1}) and (xp_{k-1}, p_{k-1}).

Now that we have found the orthogonal polynomials $p_k(x)$, we can say what the points x_i^k must be, namely, they are the roots of p_k, that is, $p_k(x_i^k) = 0$, $i = 1, 2, \ldots, k$. It follows from Theorem 4.1 that

$$p_k(x) = \prod_{i=1}^{k} (x - x_i^k) , \qquad k = 1, 2, \ldots, n .$$

The Gaussian quadrature problem is solved, except for one thing. We must show that the roots x_i^k of p_k are real numbers which lie in the interval (0, 1), otherwise the formula $\sum a_i f(x_i)$ will not make sense.

Theorem 5.1. For each $n > 1$, the zeros of $p_n(x)$ are real, distinct, and lie in (0, 1).

Proof. Since p_n is orthogonal to the polynomial 1, $\int_0^1 p_n(x)w(x)\,dx = 0$. Since $w(x) > 0$, there must be a point x_1, $0 < x_1 < 1$, at which $p_n(x)$ changes sign. Let m be the total number of points at which p_n changes sign in (0, 1), and let the points be $x_1, x_2, \ldots, x_m$. We have just shown that $m \geq 1$, and certainly $m \leq n$. Suppose $m < n$. Since p_n is orthogonal to every polynomial of degree less than n,

$$\int_0^1 p_n(x)(x - x_1) \cdots (x - x_m)w(x)\,dx = 0 .$$

But this is impossible since $p_n(x)$ changes sign at exactly those points at which $(x - x_1) \cdots (x - x_m)$ changes sign; in other words, the integrand above has one sign. This contradiction is relieved only if $m = n$.

In the exercises we show that once the $p_k(x)$ and their roots have been found the coefficients a_i in (5.2–1) can be determined without additional integrations.

The polynomials p_k, weights a_i, and roots x_i^k have been tabulated for specific weight functions $w(x)$. In case $w(x) \equiv 1$, the polynomials, apart from a constant factor and replacement of x by $2x - 1$, are called Legendre polynomials.

Constructing the Gaussian quadrature formula for any given weight $w(x)$ requires a capability for finding the roots of a polynomial. For arbitrary polynomials this is a difficult problem which is a subject for an advanced course in numerical analysis. In this case, since the roots are real and distinct, Newton's method or the method of false position will work in principle, although in practice difficulties can arise. A more elementary, less efficient, but safer procedure is the method of bisection. First, divide [0, 1] into subintervals of equal length so small that no subinterval can contain more than two roots of $p_k(x)$ (this has to be estimated somehow). Then search the sequence of consecutive endpoints for the first adjacent pair at which $p_k(x)$ has different signs. The corresponding subinterval is then divided into two equal parts; the half with endpoints at which $p_k(x)$ changes sign is divided in half, and so on. However, the translation of even this simple method into a foolproof computer algorithm is not trivial, because of the need to allow for errors made in calculating $p_k(x)$.

Numerical examples of the relative accuracy of Gaussian quadrature, Simpson's rule, and others can be found in Ralston (1965). Gaussian quadrature can be expected to be very accurate for functions which are very well approximated by polynomials of low degree, but there are other functions for which other integration rules are more accurate. For example, Exercise (1) shows that the trapezoidal rule will be excellent for functions closely approximated by trigonometric polynomials of low order.

5.3 THE ERROR OF INTEGRATION RULES

Error estimates can be obtained for specific classes of integration rules. These are derived in Wendroff (1966), for example, for Newton-Cates and Gaussian quadrature. For our purposes, it is more illuminating to extend the method of the last part of Section 4.4.

Consider any integration rule

$$\int_a^b f(x)\,dx \cong \sum_{i=1}^{n} a_i f(x_i)\,,$$

and put

$$\int_a^b f(x)\,dx - \sum_{i=1}^{n} a_i f(x_i) = E\,. \tag{5.3-1}$$

The error E is a number. If the interval of integration and the integration formulas are kept fixed, then the value of E depends on the function f,

$$E = E(f)\,.$$

Any correspondence which assigns to any function a number is called a *functional.* It is easy to see that if α and β are numbers, then

(5.3–2) $$E(\alpha f + \beta g) = \alpha E(f) + \beta E(g)\,.$$

When this situation occurs, the functional, in this case E, is called a *linear functional.*

The integration rules we have considered in this chapter all have the following property: There exists an integer m such that the rule is exact for polynomials of degree m. Thus

(5.3–3) $$E(P) = 0\,, \qquad P \text{ a polynomial of degree } m.$$

Now, according to Taylor's Theorem,

$$f(x) = \sum_{k=0}^{m} f^{(k)}(a)\,\frac{(x-a)^k}{k!} + \int_a^x \frac{(x-t)^m}{m!}\, f^{(m+1)}(t)\,dt\,.$$

Therefore, by (5.3–2), (5.3–3),

$$E(f) = E(g)\,.$$

where

$$g(x) = \int_a^x \frac{(x-t)^m}{m!}\, f^{(m+1)}(t)\,dt\,.$$

Let

(5.3–4) $$K_m(x, t) = \begin{cases} \dfrac{(x-t)^m}{m!}\,, & a \le t \le x\,, \\ 0\,, & \text{otherwise}\,. \end{cases}$$

Then

$$g(x) = \int_a^b K_m(x, t) f^{(m+1)}(t)\,dt\,.$$

It now follows that

(5.3–5) $$E(f) = \int_a^b E\big(K_m(\cdot, t)\big) f^{(m+1)}(t)\,dt\,.$$

This is a special case of the Peano Kernel Theorem. See P. J. Davis (1965). To see this we simply note that the finite sum can certainly be interchanged with the integration, and the two integrals can be interchanged as long as they each make sense.

Thus, we again have only to compute the error for a specific function in order to obtain the error for any function (with enough derivatives). For example, for the trapezoidal rule,

$$E\big(K_1(\cdot, t)\big) = \frac{(x_{i+1} - t)(x_i - t)}{2}\,, \qquad x_i \le t \le x_{i+1}\,,$$

and

$$E(f) = \sum \int_{x_i}^{x_{i+1}} \frac{(x_{i+1} - t)(x_i - t)}{2} f''(t)\, dt$$

$$= -\frac{h^2}{12}(b - a)f''(\xi), \qquad a < \xi < b.$$

Simpson's rule and the trapezoidal rule with endpoint correction also yield to this analysis (Exercises 7, 10). In principle, so do the other rules, but the computation of $E(K_m)$ is much harder.

EXERCISES

Section 5.1

1. Let $x_j = -\pi + j\pi/N$, $j = 0, 1, \ldots, 2N$. Let

$$T(f) = \frac{\pi}{N} \sum_0^{2N-1} \frac{1}{2} [f(x_j) + f(x_{j+1})].$$

Prove that $T(\cos kx) = 0$, $0 < k < N$.

Section 5.2

2. Prove that $(xp_{n-1}, p_{n-2}) = ||p_{n-1}||^2$.
3. Prove that p_k and p_{k-1} have no common roots.
4. Let $\bar{p}_k(x) = ||p_k||^{-1} p_k(x)$, let $r_k = ||p_k||$, and let

$$\Delta_k(x, y) = \bar{p}_k(x)\bar{p}_{k-1}(y) - \bar{p}_k(y)\bar{p}_{k-1}(x).$$

Prove that

$$\frac{r_{k+1}}{r_k} \Delta_{k+1} = (x - y)\bar{p}_k(x)\bar{p}_k(y) + \frac{r_k}{r_{k-1}} \Delta_k,$$

and that

$$\frac{r_{n+1}}{r_n} \Delta_{n+1}(x, y) = \sum_0^n (x - y)\bar{p}_k(x)\bar{p}_k(y).$$

5. Let $\rho_j = \sum_{k=0}^{n-1} [\bar{p}_k(x_j)]^2$, where the x_j are the zeros of $p_n(x)$. Use the previous exercise to show that

$$\rho_j^{-1} \sum_0^{n-1} \bar{p}_k(x)\bar{p}_k(x_j) = \delta_j(x),$$

and that

$$a_j = \int_0^1 \delta_j(x) w(x)\, dx = \rho_j^{-1}.$$

6. Write a program to compute the first five polynomials orthogonal on $[-1, 1]$ (Legendre polynomials) Find x_1^5.

Section 5.3

7. Show that the error in the trapezoidal rule with endpoint correction is

$$\sum \int_{x_i}^{x_{i+1}} \tfrac{1}{24}(x_{i+1} - t)^2 (x_i - t)^2 f^{(4)}(t)\, dt \; .$$

8. Let $f(x)$ be a continuously differentiable function for which there is no information about $f''(x)$, but $|f'(x)| \leq M$, $a \leq x \leq b$. Show that the error in the trapezoidal rule is at most $\frac{1}{4}(b - a)Mb$ (*)

9. Let $\sum_{i=1}^{n} a_i f(x_i)$ be an integration rule which is exact for polynomials of degree m, on $[a, b]$. Show that

$$E(f) = \frac{1}{m!} \int_a^b \lambda(t) f^{(m+1)}(t)\, dt \; ,$$

where

$$\lambda(t) = \frac{1}{m+1}(b - t)^{m+1} - \sum_{x_i > t} a_i (x_i - t)^m \; .$$

10. Without using Chapter 2, prove that Simpson's rule is exact for cubics, and rederive the integral representation for the error.

8. Write $f(x) = \frac{f(a)+f(b)}{2} + \frac{x-a}{2} f'(\xi) + \frac{x-b}{2} f'(\eta)$

$a < \xi < x < \eta < b$, by Taylor's theorem.

So $E = \left(\int_a^b f\right) - (b-a)\frac{f(b)+f(a)}{2} = \int_a^b \left[\frac{x-a}{2} f'(\xi) + \frac{x-b}{2} f'(\eta)\right] dx$; so

$|E| \leq \frac{M}{2}(b-a)^2 < \frac{M}{4} b(b-a)$ when $b < 2a$

(Notice this does not even require f to be twice differentiable.)

Assuming (*), we get

$|E| \leq M \cdot \frac{b-a}{2} \cdot \min\left\{\frac{b}{2}, b-a\right\}$

Notice that the estimate (*) has some "drawbacks":

Translation reduces error bd to nonsense

(a) $b = 0$

(b) if $b = 10^6$, $b = 1$ $(b-a = 1)$

Chapter Six

APPLICATIONS OF INTERPOLATION, PART 2

APPLICATIONS OF INTERPOLATION, PART 2

In this chapter we show how interpolating methods are used to find roots of functions, to solve ordinary differential equations, and to obtain approximate values of a function. Since convergence proofs and error estimates for these methods are somewhat more difficult than for the other methods considered in this book, we have referred the reader to other texts for most of the purely mathematical aspects of these methods.

6.1 MULTI-POINT METHODS

We reconsider here the problem of solving the equation

$$f(x) = 0 \,. \tag{6.1-1}$$

A direct use of interpolation might proceed as follows: compute $f(x_i) = f_i$, $i = 1, 2, \ldots, k$, and then replace $f(x)$ by $\sum f_i \delta_i(x)$. Unfortunately, finding a root of the latter function is nearly as difficult as for the original function. Because of this, multi-point methods are based on a process known as inverse interpolation.

We assume that there is an inverse function $g(y)$, that is to say, a function $g(y)$ such that

$$g\big(f(x)\big) = x \,.$$

Now, suppose $f(\alpha) = 0$. Then

$$\alpha = g\big(f(\alpha)\big) = g(0) \,.$$

Thus the problem of solving (6.1–1) is the same as that of evaluating $g(0)$. The multi-point method replaces $g(y)$ by

$$P(y) = \sum_{i=1}^{k} g(y_i)\delta_i(y) \,,$$

and correspondingly, $g(0)$ by

$$\begin{aligned} P(0) &= \sum g(y_i)\delta_i(0) \\ &= \sum g(y_i) \prod_{j \neq i} \left(\frac{-y_j}{y_i - y_j} \right). \end{aligned}$$

If we put $y_i = f_i = f(x_i)$, then

$$P(0) = \sum x_i \prod_{j \neq i} \frac{-f_j}{f_i - f_j}. \tag{6.1-2}$$

$P(0)$ is an approximation to the desired root α. A common use of this approximation is in an iteration based on (6.1–2), namely,

$$x_{n+k+1} = \sum_{i=1}^{k} x_{n+i} \prod_{j \neq i} \frac{-f_{n+j}}{f_{n+i} - f_{n+j}}. \tag{6.1-3}$$

A special and important case of this iteration occurs when $k = 2$, for then, after re-indexing the x_i,

$$x_{k+1} = x_k \frac{-f_{k-1}}{f_k - f_{k-1}} + x_{k-1} \frac{-f_k}{f_{k-1} - f_k}.$$

It is easily seen that

$$x_{k+1} = x_k - \frac{f_k}{\dfrac{f_k - f_{k-1}}{x_k - x_{k-1}}}.$$

which is just the method of false position described in Exercise 3.2.

The method of false position is very useful, and indeed, in a sense to be described, is better than Newton's method. First, note that if in each step of the iteration we save $f(x_{k-1})$ from the preceding, then we only have to evaluate $f(x_k)$, that is, the method of false position requires one functional evaluation at each iteration. Newton's method has two functional evaluations, $f(x_k)$ and $f'(x_k)$. In general, Newton's method takes twice as much time as the method of false position, *per iteration*. The question we have to answer is, does the method of false position take more, or less, than twice as many iterations as Newton's method to produce an answer. If less, then it is preferable to Newton's method.

Recall that in Chapter 3 we showed that if e_i is the error (suitably defined) at the ith step of Newton's method, then

$$e_i \leq e_0^{(2^i)}.$$

Suppose $e_0 < 1$. Then $e_i \leq 10^{-p}e_0$ if

$$e_0^{(2^i)} = 10^{-p}e_0.$$

Taking logarithms twice we have

$$i \log 2 = \log\left[\frac{-p + \log e_0}{\log e_0}\right] \equiv c\,.$$

Thus, if i_N is the number of iterations needed to reduce the initial error by 10^{-p},

$$i_N = \frac{c}{\log 2}\,.$$

Now it can be shown [Ostrowski (1960)] that if d_i is a suitably defined measure of the error at the ith step in the method of false position, then for large i

$$d_i \le d_0^{(r^i)}\,,$$

where

$$r = \frac{1+\sqrt{5}}{2}\,.$$

If we assume that $d_0 = e_0$, and define i_R to be the number of iterations needed to reduce e_0 to $10^{-p}e_0$, then

$$i_R = \frac{c}{\log r} \qquad \text{so that} \qquad \frac{i_R}{i_N} = \frac{\log 2}{\log r}\,.$$

But in fact, $\log 2/\log r < 2$, so

$$i_R < 2i_N\,.$$

Thus, in general, but of course not in every specific case, the method of false position is faster than Newton's method.

For a complete discussion of multi-point methods see Traub (1964).

6.2 MULTI-STEP METHODS FOR ORDINARY DIFFERENTIAL EQUATIONS

Consider the differential equation

$$\frac{dy}{dx} = f(x, y)\,, \tag{6.2–1}$$

$$y(x_0) = y_0\,.$$

As in Chapter 3, we will seek an approximate solution at mesh points $x_0 < x_1 \cdots < x_i < \cdots$. It follows from (6.2–1) that

$$y(x_{n+1}) = y(x_{n-r}) + \int_{x_{n-r}}^{x_{n+1}} f(x, y)\,dx \tag{6.2–2}$$

for $r \geq 0$. Now, let Y_i be the approximate values of $y(x_i)$. Choose $s \geq 0$, and let $P(x)$ be the Lagrange interpolating polynomial taking on the values $f(x_i, Y_i)$ at the x_i, $i = n - s, n - s + 1, \ldots, n + 1$, that is,

$$P(x) = \sum_{i=n-s}^{n+1} f(x_i, Y_i)\delta_i(x) ,$$

where here

$$\delta_i(x) = \prod_{\substack{j=n-s \\ j \neq i}}^{n+1} \frac{x - x_j}{x_i - x_j} .$$

Putting

$$\beta_i = \int_{x_{n-r}}^{x_{n+1}} \delta_i(x)\, dx ,$$

we replace (6.2–2) by

$$Y_{n+1} = Y_{n-r} + \sum_{i=n-s}^{n+1} \beta_i f(x_i, Y_i) . \tag{6.2–3}$$

This formula is the basic form of multi-step methods. However, it cannot be used as it stands, because Y_{n+1} appears as an argument in the right side. Equation (6.2–3) is an implicit multi-step formula. An explicit multi-step formula can be obtained by not using x_{n+1} as one of the interpolation points. Using such a formula we can *predict* the value of Y_{n+1} by an equation such as the following:

$$\bar{Y}_{n+1} = Y_{n-p} + \sum_{i=n-\sigma}^{n} \alpha_i f(x_i, Y_i) . \tag{6.2–4}$$

$\bar{Y}_{n+1}$ is the predicted value of Y_{n+1}. A *corrected* value is obtained by setting

$$Y_{n+1} = Y_{n-r} + \sum_{i=n-s}^{n} \beta_i f(x_i, Y_i) + \beta_{n+1} f(x_{n+1}, \bar{Y}_{n+1}) . \tag{6.2–5}$$

The above pair of formulas is called a predictor-corrector method.

If for the exact solution $y(x)$,

$$y_{n+1} = y_{n-r} + \sum \beta_i f(x_i, y_i) + O(h^{p+1}) ,$$

where $h = \max |x_i - x_{i-1}|$, then the multi-step method is said to have order p. If (6.2–3) has order p, and (6.2–4) has order $p - 1$, then the predictor-corrector pair (6.2–4), (6.2–5) produces an approximation Y_i such that

$$\max_i |y_i - Y_i| \leq \text{const } h^p .$$

A proof of this, and a complete discussion of multi-step methods is given by Henrici (1962a, 1962b).

A popular predictor-corrector is the following (for equal intervals, $x_i - x_{i-1} = h$),

$$\bar{Y}_{n+1} = Y_n + \frac{h}{24}[-9f(Y_{n-3}) + 37f(Y_{n-2}) - 59f(Y_{n-1}) + 55f(Y_n)], \tag{6.2-6}$$

$$Y_{n+1} = Y_n + \frac{h}{24}[f(Y_{n-2}) - 5f(Y_{n-1}) + 19f(Y_n) + 9f(\bar{Y}_{n+1})]. \tag{6.2-7}$$

For this pair, $p = 4$. It is called Adams' method.

There are two basic computational differences between single step and predictor-corrector methods. The latter, no matter what p is, require only two functional evaluations per point, namely $f(Y_n)$ and $f(\bar{Y}_{n+1})$. It has even been suggested that wherever Y_i appears as an argument of f in (6.2–4) and (6.2–5) that $\bar{Y}_i$ be substituted [see Wendroff (1966), p. 106]. In this case only one functional evaluation need be performed at each step. For single step methods the number of functional evaluations increases with p. For example, the fourth order Runge-Kutta uses four functional evaluations.

The other difference is the fact that the single step methods are self-starting, and one easily changes mesh size. Adams' method, for example, can only start at x_3, so Y_1, Y_2, Y_3 must be obtained by other means, perhaps Runge-Kutta. Any point at which h is to be changed must be treated as a new starting point. This makes the programming of a predictor-corrector method awkward, but that cannot be considered a serious objection in a problem for which it is essential to minimize computing time.

6.3 LEAST SQUARES POLYNOMIAL APPROXIMATION

There are ways other than direct interpolation to obtain approximating polynomials. One of these is least squares: we seek to replace $f(x)$ on the interval $[a, b]$ by a polynomial $P(x)$ of degree n with the following property:

$$\int_a^b [f(x) - P(x)]^2\,dx \leq \int_a^b [f(x) - Q(x)]^2\,dx, \tag{6.3-1}$$

where $Q(x)$ is *any* polynomial of degree n. We will solve this by supposing that such a polynomial $P(x)$ exists, then finding conditions that $P(x)$ must satisfy and then using these conditions to demonstrate the existence of P. Assuming the existence of P, we can set $Q = P + R$, where we may now take R to be an arbitrary polynomial of degree n. Then from (6.3–1),

$$\int_a^b R^2\,dx + 2\int_a^b R(P - f)\,dx \geq 0\,. \tag{6.3–2}$$

Now, it is necessary that

$$\int_a^b R(P - f)\,dx = 0 \tag{6.3–3}$$

for all R, for if not then there surely exists an R such that

$$\int_a^b R(P - f)\,dx < 0\,,$$

and therefore,

$$\int_a^b R^2\,dx - 2\left|\int_a^b R(P - f)\,dx\right| \geq 0\,.$$

This leads to a contradiction if we replace R by αR, where

$$\alpha = \frac{\left|\int_a^b R(P - f)\,dx\right|}{\int_a^b R^2\,dx}\,.$$

Thus, (6.3–3) is necessary and sufficient for (6.3–1). It also follows from (6.3–3) that P is unique, for suppose there were another such polynomial P'. Then

$$\int_a^b R(P' - f)\,dx = 0\,,$$

and by subtraction

$$\int_a^b (P' - P)R\,dx = 0\,.$$

This is true for any R, in particular for $R = P' - P$, that is,

$$\int_a^b (P' - P)^2\,dx = 0 \qquad \text{or} \qquad P'(x) = P(x)\,.$$

Equation (6.3–3) can be used in several ways to find P. One way is to put

$$P(x) = \sum_{i=0}^{n} a_i x^i$$

and then successively put $R = 1, x, x^2, \ldots, x^n$. This leads to the following system of equations:

$$\sum_j r_{ij} a_j = b_i\,, \qquad i = 0(1)n\,, \tag{6.3–4}$$

where

$$r_{ij} = \int_a^b x^{i+j}\,dx \qquad \text{and} \qquad b_i = \int_a^b f(x)x^i\,dx\,.$$

This system can be solved by the method described in the next chapter.

Orthogonal polynomials provide a second means of representing the solution of the least squares problem. According to Section 5.2 there exist polynomials $p_k(x)$ such that the degree of $p_k(x)$ is k, and such that

$$\int_a^b p_i(x)p_j(x)\,dx = \begin{cases} 1\,, & i = j\,, \\ 0\,, & i \neq j\,. \end{cases}$$

Put

$$P(x) = \sum_{i=0}^{n} a_i p_i(x)\,.$$

Since any polynomial R of degree n can be expressed as a linear combination of the p_i, we need only satisfy (6.3–3) for $R = p_0, p_1, \ldots, p_n$. But

$$\int_a^b (f - P)p_i(x)\,dx = \int_a^b fp_i\,dx - a_i\,.$$

Thus,

$$P(x) = \sum_{i=0}^{n} \left[\int_a^b f(x)p_i(x)\,dx\right] p_i(x)\,,$$

solves the least squares problem.

For further reading on the theory of approximation we suggest texts by Davis (1965), and Rice (1964).

6.4 APPROXIMATION BY INTERPOLATION

In Section 4.3 it was indicated that Lagrange interpolation using equidistant nodes is an unreliable method of approximating functions. It has been observed that there does exist a set of nodes which is "good" for any continuously differentiable function. Suppose we wish to approximate $f(x)$ on the interval $[-1, 1]$, using a polynomial $P_n(x)$ of degee n. We use the Chebyshev nodes

$$\lambda_k^{(n+1)} = \cos\left(\frac{2k-1}{2(n+1)}\pi\right), \qquad k = 1, 2, \ldots, n+1\,.$$

Then if $f'(x)$ is continuous on $[-1, 1]$,

$$\lim_{n\to\infty} \max_{-1\leq x\leq 1} |f(x) - P_n(x)| = 0\,.$$

[See Wendroff (1966).] In Fig. 6.1 we show how well this method works for the function $(1 + 25x^2)^{-1}$, in contrast to equidistant interpolation.

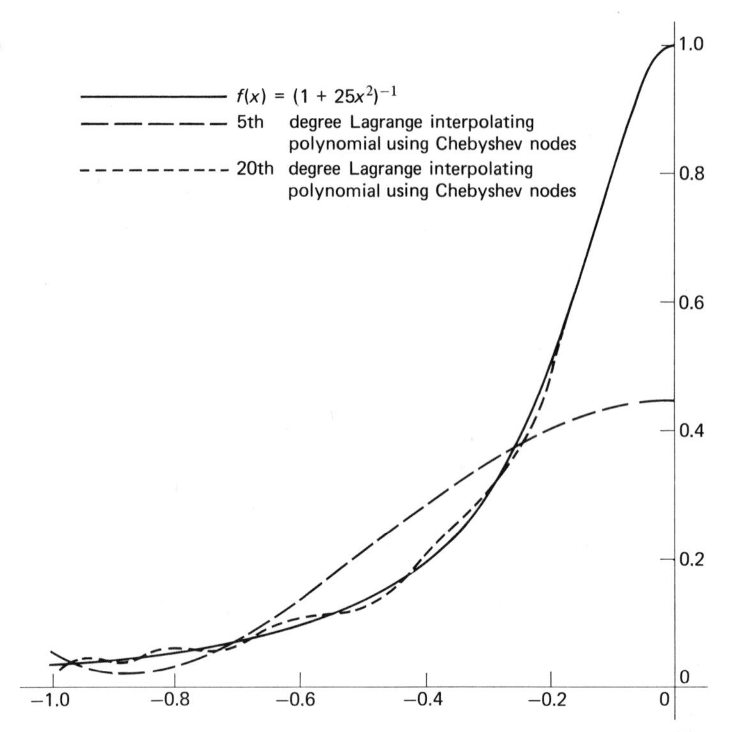

Figure 6.1

see p. 63

EXERCISES

Section 6.1

1. (Iterated interpolation). Let $x_{i_1}, x_{i_2}, \ldots, x_{i_n}$ be n distinct points and let $P_{i_1,\ldots,i_n}(x)$ be the Lagrange interpolating polynomial of degree $n - 1$ such that

$$P_{i_1,\ldots,i_n}(x_{i_\nu}) = f(x_{i_\nu}), \qquad \nu = 1, 2, \ldots, n.$$

Prove that if x_j, x_k, and x_{i_ν}, $\nu = 1(1)m$, are any $m + 2$ distinct points, then

$$p_{i_1,i_2,\ldots,i_m,j,k}(x) = \frac{(x - x_k)P_{i_1,\ldots,i_m,j}(x) - (x - x_j)P_{i_1,\ldots,i_m,k}(x)}{x_j - x_k}.$$

2. Set up a scheme for evaluating the Lagrange interpolating polynomial for an arbitrary number of points which uses only linear interpolation and Exercise 1.
3. Construct an algorithm to perform the most general multi-point iteration. Use Exercise 2.

Section 6.2

5. Write a flow diagram to integrate an arbitrary first-order differential equation by an arbitrary predictor-corrector. Assume the coefficients of the predictor-corrector formulas are given. Assume also that all necessary initial data is given.

Section 6.3

5. Prove that the polynomial P which satisfies (6.3–3) actually minimizes the right side of (6.3–1).
6. Construct a theory of least squares approximation analogous to that given in Section 6.3 for the following: given distinct points $x_1, \ldots, x_k$, and data $y_1, \ldots, y_k$, to find the polynomial $P(x)$ of degree n such that

$$\sum_{i=1}^{k} [y_i - P(x_i)]^2 \leq \sum_{i=1}^{k} [y_i - Q(x_i)]^2$$

for all polynomials $Q(x)$ of degree n.

7. Solve Exercise 6 explicitly for $k = 3$, $n = 2$.

Chapter Seven

GAUSSIAN ELIMINATION

7.1 Formal Reduction to Triangular Form

7.2 Pivoting

7.3 Scaling and Uncertainty

7.4 The Full Algorithm

GAUSSIAN ELIMINATION

In the preceding six chapters we discussed methods of obtaining approximations, in a finite number of operations, for some of the continuous processes of analysis. In this chapter we describe a method for solving a linear system of equations. This is already a finite problem, since Cramer's rule provides the solution in a finite number of steps, so the reader may wonder why any further investigation is necessary. There are two reasons, one being speed. Cramer's rule, with determinants evaluated by expanding in minors, takes on the order of $n!$ multiplications to solve a system of n equations in n unknowns. If $n = 20$, and one multiplication takes 10^{-6} seconds, the time required would be several million years. The second reason is the loss of accuracy caused by floating point, fixed word length, arithmetic. Gaussian elimination with row interchanges solves both these problems.

7.1 FORMAL REDUCTION TO TRIANGULAR FORM

We are looking for a method to solve a linear system of equations:

$$
\begin{aligned}
a_{11}x_1 + a_{12}x_2 + \cdots + a_{1n}x_n &= b_1 , \\
a_{21}x_1 + a_{22}x_2 \quad \cdots + a_{2n}x_n &= b_2 , \\
&\vdots \\
a_{n1}x_1 + \quad \cdots + a_{nn}x_n &= b_n .
\end{aligned}
\tag{7.1-1}
$$

In Chapter 4 we have already dealt with two special cases of such a system. One had the following form:

$$
\begin{aligned}
a_{11}x_1 + a_{12}x_2 + \cdots + a_{1n}x_n &= b_1 , \\
a_{22}x_2 + \cdots + a_{2n}x_n &= b_2 , \\
&\ddots \\
a_{nn}x_n &= b_n .
\end{aligned}
\tag{7.1-2}
$$

Such a system is called triangular. The solution is found by first solving the last equation for x_n,

$$x_n = \frac{b_n}{a_{nn}},$$

then solving the next to last equation for x_{n-1},

$$x_{n-1} = \frac{1}{a_{n-1,n-1}}(b_{n-1} - a_{n-1,n}x_n),$$

and so on. The complete algorithm is

$$\text{(7.1–3)} \qquad \begin{array}{l} \text{For } k = 1(1)n, \\ \quad i = n - k + 1, \\ \quad x_i = (a_{ii})^{-1}\left(b_i - \sum_{j=i+1}^{n} a_{ij}x_j\right). \end{array}$$

We have used the convention $\sum_{n+1}^{n} a_{ij}x_j = 0$.

Another linear system we have already solved arose in 4.3 in obtaining interpolating splines. There we had a system of the following type:

$$\text{(7.1–4)} \qquad \begin{aligned} a_{11}x_1 + a_{12}x_2 \qquad\qquad\qquad &= b_1, \\ a_{21}x_1 + a_{22}x_2 + a_{23}x_3 \qquad &= b_2, \\ a_{32}x_2 + a_{33}x_3 + a_{34}x_4 &= b_3, \\ &\;\;\vdots \\ a_{n,n-1}x_{n-1} + a_{nn}x_n &= b_n. \end{aligned}$$

The technique we used was to eliminate x_1 from the second equation, x_2 from the third equation, and so on. When this is completed the following system results:

$$\text{(7.1–5)} \qquad \begin{aligned} x_1 - p_1x_2 \qquad\qquad\qquad &= q_1, \\ x_2 - p_2x_3 \qquad\quad &= q_2, \\ x_3 - p_3x_4 &= q_3, \\ \ddots \qquad & \\ x_n &= q_n, \end{aligned}$$

with

$$p_1 = -\frac{a_{12}}{a_{11}}, \qquad q_1 = \frac{b_1}{a_{11}},$$

$$p_i = \frac{-a_{i,i+1}}{a_{i,i-1}p_{i-1} + a_{ii}}, \qquad q_i = \frac{b_i - a_{i,i-1}q_{i-1}}{a_{i,i-1}p_{i-1} + a_{ii}}.$$

The system (7.1–4) is called tridiagonal, and the method of solution was to find a triangular system, (7.1–5), with the same solution as the original systems. For complete systems (7.1–1) the generalization of this process of finding an equivalent triangular system is called triangular decomposition. We systematically eliminate x_1 from equations 2, 3, . . . , n. Then we eliminate x_2 from equations 3, 4, . . . , n, and so on. Now this elimination process never does anything to the unknown x_i, since it only operates on the coefficients a_{ij} and the b_i. We might just as well write the coefficients in an array,

$$\begin{bmatrix} a_{11} & a_{12} \cdots a_{1n} \\ a_{21} & a_{22} \cdots a_{2n} \\ \vdots & \vdots \\ a_{n1} & \cdots a_{nn} \end{bmatrix} \tag{7.1–6}$$

and then proceed just as if we had written (7.1–1). Such an array is called a matrix, in this case an $n \times n$ matrix. The matrix can be represented by a single symbol A,

$$A = \{a_{ij}\} .$$

The ith row of A is $(a_{i1}, a_{i2}, \ldots, a_{in})$, the jth column of A is $(a_{1j}, a_{2j}, \ldots, a_{nj})$.

The n-tuple of unknowns, $(x_1, x_2, \ldots, x_n)$ is called a vector, which we can represent by the symbol x,

$$x = (x_1, x_2, \ldots, x_n) .$$

Likewise, we may put

$$b = (b_1, b_2, \ldots, b_n) .$$

We now define a new vector Ax as follows:

$$(Ax)_i \equiv i\text{th component of } Ax \equiv \sum a_{ij}x_j .$$

With this the system (7.1–1) may be condensed to

$$Ax = b . \tag{7.1–7}$$

To proceed with the triangular decomposition, suppose $a_{11} \neq 0$, and let

$$m_{i1} = \frac{a_{i1}}{a_{11}}, \qquad i = 2(1)n , \tag{7.1–8}$$

and

(7.1–9)

For $i = 2(1)n$
  For $j = 2(1)n$
    $a_{ij}^{(2)} = a_{ij} - m_{i1}a_{1j}$,

and

$$b_i^{(2)} = b_i - m_{i1}b_1\,, \qquad i = 2(1)n\,.$$

Consider the following system:

$$\begin{array}{lrcl} & a_{11}x_1 + a_{12}x_2 & + \cdots + a_{12}x_n & = b_1\,, \\ (7.1\text{–}10) & 0 \qquad a_{22}^{(2)}x_2 & + \cdots + a_{2n}^{(2)}x_n & = b_2^{(2)}\,, \\ & \vdots & & \\ & 0 \qquad a_{n2}^{(2)}x_2 & + \cdots + a_{nn}^{(2)}x_n & = b_n^{(2)}\,. \end{array}$$

This system has the same solution as the original, since we have done nothing more than subtract from the ith equation the first equation multiplied by m_{i1}.

We may now temporarily forget the first equation and consider as a new problem the system

$$\sum_{j=2}^{n} a_{ij}^{(2)}x_j = b_i^{(2)}\,, \qquad i = 2(1)n\,.$$

We repeat the elimination process on this system, this time eliminating x_2. Thus, putting

$$m_{i2} = \frac{a_{i2}^{(2)}}{a_{22}^{(2)}}\,, \qquad i = 3(1)n\,,$$

For $i = 3(1)n$

  For $j = 3(1)n$

    $a_{ij}^{(3)} = a_{ij}^{(2)} - m_{i2}a_{2j}^{(2)}\,,$

$$b_i^{(3)} = b_i^{(2)} - m_{i2}b_2^{(2)}\,, \qquad i = 3(1)n\,,$$

we again obtain a new system which has the same solution as the original, namely,

$$\begin{array}{l} a_{11}x_1 + a_{12}x_2 + \cdots + a_{1n}x_n = b_1\,, \\ 0 + a_{22}^{(2)}x_2 + \cdots + a_{2n}^{(2)}x_n = b_2^{(2)}\,, \\ 0 + 0 + a_{33}^{(3)}x_3 + \cdots + a_{3n}^{(3)}x_n = b_3^{(3)}\,, \\ \vdots \qquad \vdots \qquad \qquad \vdots \\ 0 \quad\; 0 + a_{n3}^{(3)}x_3 + \cdots + a_{nn}^{(3)}x_n = b_n^{(3)}\,. \end{array}$$

The full decomposition algorithm is now clear: putting

$$\{a_{ij}^{(1)}\} = \{a_{ij}\}\,,\ \{b_i^{(1)}\} = \{b_i\}\,,$$

we have,

$$
\begin{array}{l}
\text{For } k = 1(1)n-1 \\
\quad \text{For } i = k+1(1)n \\
\quad\quad m_{ik} = \dfrac{a_{ik}^{(k)}}{a_{kk}^{(k)}} \\
\quad\quad \text{For } j = k+1(1)n \\
\quad\quad\quad a_{ij}^{(k+1)} = a_{ij}^{(k)} - m_{ik}a_{kj}^{(k)} ,
\end{array}
$$

$$
\begin{array}{l}
\text{For } k = 1(1)n-1 \\
\quad \text{For } i = k+1(1)n \\
\quad\quad b_i^{(k+1)} = b_i^{(k)} - m_{ik}b_k^{(k)} .
\end{array}
$$

Of course, this is purely formal, since there is no guarantee that $a_{kk}^{(k)} \neq 0$. However, if we make this assumption, then we have succeeded in reducing the original system to the equivalent triangular system

$$
\begin{aligned}
a_{11}x_1 + a_{12}x_2 + \cdots + a_{1n}x_n &= b_1 , \\
a_{22}^{(2)}x_2 + \cdots + a_{2n}^{(2)}x_n &= b_2^{(2)} , \\
a_{33}^{(3)} + \cdots + a_{3n}^{(3)}x_n &= b_3^{(3)} , \\
\ddots \qquad \vdots \qquad &\quad \vdots \\
a_{nn}^{(n)}x_n &= b_n^{(n)} .
\end{aligned} \tag{7.1-11}
$$

The triangular decomposition algorithm can be simplified somewhat if we assume that we are dealing with a copy of the given system of equations and therefore can use the memory occupied by the a_{ij} for the storage of the m_{ik} and $a_{ij}^{(k)}$. The m_{ik} (called multipliers) can be stored where the zeros occur, and the $a_{ij}^{(k)}$can be overwritten on the old a_{ij}. The algorithm becomes

$$
\begin{array}{l}
\text{For } k = 1(1)n-1 \\
\quad \text{For } i = k+1(1)n \\
\quad\quad a_{ik} = \dfrac{a_{ik}}{a_{kk}} \\
\quad\quad \text{For } j = k+1(1)n \\
\quad\quad\quad a_{ij} = a_{ij} - a_{ik}a_{kj} ,
\end{array} \tag{7.1-12}
$$

$$
\begin{array}{l}
\text{For } k = 1(1)n-1 \\
\quad \text{For } i = k+1(1)n \\
\quad\quad b_i = b_i - a_{ik}b_k .
\end{array} \tag{7.1-13}
$$

As usual, equal signs are interpreted as substitution operations.

The three algorithms (7.1–12), (7.1–13), and (7.1–3) are the basic steps in Gaussian elimination. Assuming that the $a_{kk}^{(k)}$ do not vanish, we have solved the problem of obtaining an efficient method for solving linear systems. By summing over the loops in (7.1–12) we can easily count the number of multiplications or divisions involved in that algorithm, it being customary to count only those operations. Calling this number C_n we have

$$\begin{aligned} C_n &= \sum_{k=1}^{n-1} \sum_{k+1}^{n} \left[\left(\sum_{k+1}^{n} 1 \right) + 1 \right] \\ &= \sum_{k=1}^{n-1} (n - k + 1)(n - k) . \end{aligned}$$

This can be evaluated using the formulas for the sums of succesive integers and squares of integers. We find that

$$\lim_{n \to \infty} n^{-3} C_n = \tfrac{1}{3} .$$

The contribution from (7.1–13), (7.1–3) is of order n^2 and can be neglected. Thus, for large n triangular decomposition requires $n^3/3$ operations, a considerable improvement over $n!$.

7.2 PIVOTING

Since the triangular decomposition method for solving linear systems cannot be performed with exact arithmetic, one might expect that there will be an accumulation of error for large systems which will put definite limits on the size of the system which can be handled. The fact is that this error growth is so explosive that a completely bad answer can be obtained even for a system of two equations. Consider the following:

$$\begin{aligned} \varepsilon x_1 + x_2 &= 1 - r , \\ x_1 + x_2 &= 1 . \end{aligned} \tag{7.2–1}$$

From the decomposition algorithm we obtain

$$\left(1 - \frac{1}{\varepsilon}\right) x_2 = 1 - \frac{1 - r}{\varepsilon} .$$

Now, if ε is very small, floating point fixed word length arithmetic will result in

$$1 - \frac{1}{\varepsilon} = \frac{-1}{\varepsilon}, \qquad 1 - \frac{1-r}{\varepsilon} = \frac{-(1-r)}{\varepsilon}, \qquad \text{or} \qquad x_2 = 1 - r .$$

The first equation then gives

$$x_1 = 0 .$$

However, the exact solution is

$$x_2 = \frac{1 - r - \varepsilon}{1 - \varepsilon},$$

which is close to $1 - r$, but

$$x_1 = \frac{r}{1 - \varepsilon},$$

which is close to r, not 0. A specific example of this type is given by Forsythe and Moler (1967).

We can see both the reason for the difficulty and a possible cure by interchanging the order of the equations in (7.2–1). We now have

$$\begin{aligned} x_1 + x_2 &= 1 , \\ \varepsilon x_1 + x_2 &= 1 - r , \end{aligned} \tag{7.2-2}$$

and reduction to triangular form produces

$$(1 - \varepsilon)x_2 = 1 - r - \varepsilon .$$

Again, for small ε

$$1 - \varepsilon = 1 , \qquad 1 - r - \varepsilon = 1 - r ,$$

so

$$x_2 = 1 - r .$$

Now, however, the first equation produces

$$x_1 = r ,$$

which is much better.

In the second case the new coefficients of the second equation are obtained by adding a small quantity to the old coefficients. In the first case the new coefficients of the second equation are obtained by adding to the old coefficients a quantity so large that the floating point addition causes a complete loss of the information contained in that equation. In general, when forming

$$a_{ij}^{(2)} = a_{ij} - m_{i1}a_{1j} ,$$

if $|m_{i1}a_{1j}|$ is very much greater than $|a_{ij}|$ then a loss of information contained in a_{ij} will result. This was controlled in the example above by reordering the equations so that $|m_{i1}|$ was small, and this is the procedure that has been found to be effective for the systems of equations arising in practice.

In general, we search the numbers $|a_{i1}|$, $i = 1, 2, \ldots, n$ for the largest. Suppose this occurs at $i = \sigma_1$, that is,

$$|a_{\sigma_1 1}| = \max_{1 \le i \le n} |a_{i1}| .$$

We now interchange the first equation with the σ_1th equation, and proceed. Now, however

$$|m_{i1}| = \left| \frac{a_{i1}}{a_{11}} \right| \le 1$$

so the magnitude of $m_{i1}a_{1j}$ is no greater than the magnitude of a_{1j}. This must be repeated for each stage of the elimination, that is, for $k = 1, 2, \ldots, n - 1$, find σ_k such that

$$|a_{\sigma_k k}^{(k)}| = \max_{k \le i \le n} |a_{ik}^{(k)}|$$

and then interchange the kth equation with the σ_kth before eliminating x_k. In this way all the multipliers will be less or equal to one in magnitude. The whole process is called *partial pivoting*, and $a_{\sigma_k k}$ is called the *pivot*.

We are now sure that the multipliers are well-defined unless at some stage

$$\max_{k \le i \le n} |a_{ik}^{(k)}| = 0 ,$$

but in that case the system is singular and we cannot proceed.

There are three classes of matrices for which partial pivoting is known to work well, even for very large n. These are (1), *strictly diagonally dominant*, that is to say, if

$$|a_{ii}| > \sum_{j \ne i} |a_{ij}| , \qquad i = 1, 2, \ldots, n ;$$

(2), *positive definite*, which means that if $\sum_{i=1}^{n} x_i^2 \ne 0$ then

$$\sum_i \sum_j a_{ij} x_i x_j > 0 ;$$

and (3), *Hessenberg*, or almost triangular, that is

$$a_{ij} = 0 , \qquad i - j \ge 2 ,$$

The first two types occur frequently in practice, and for them even the unmodified triangular decomposition is satisfactory. See Wendroff (1966) for details.

If partial pivoting gives poor results it may be possible to do better with *complete pivoting*. Suppose we have gone through the triangular decomposition algorithm to the point where we wish to eliminate x_k. Then we find integers i^*, j^* such that

$$|a_{i^*j^*}^{(k)}| = \max_{\substack{k \le i \le n \\ k \le j \le n}} |a_{ij}^{(k)}| .$$

We then interchange the i^*th and kth equations (or rows), and we also interchange the j^*th and kth columns. This puts the largest element into the pivoted position. One must keep track of the column interchanges since they involve renaming the unknowns.

J. H. Wilkinson [see Wendroff (1966)] has produced an example in which complete pivoting is better than partial pivoting. David H. Peterson (private communication) has found randomly generated matrices for which complete pivoting was very much better than partial pivoting. However, the experience of numerical analysts at this time indicates that partial pivoting with scaling, as explained in the next section, is adequate for the systems of equations occurring in practice.

7.3 SCALING AND UNCERTAINTY

The solution of the equations of a given linear system is not affected if any equation is multiplied by a constant, or *scale factor*. The presence of "hidden" scale factors can seriously influence the accuracy of the numerical solution. Consider the system

$$x_1 + \frac{1}{\varepsilon} x_2 = \frac{1 - r}{\varepsilon} ,$$

$$x_1 + x_2 = 1 ,$$

which is equivalent to (7.2–1). If we apply partial pivoting there will be no row interchange, but triangular decomposition will produce the same poor result as was obtained for (7.2–1).

At the very least, then, the introduction of scale factors, or *scaling*, can affect the choice of pivots. Scaling also has a more subtle effect. Suppose we wish to obtain the solution of the system $Ax = b$, but we perturb the elements of A and b, say $a'_{ij} = a_{ij} + \delta(a_{ij})$, $b'_i = b_i + \delta(b_i)$. Now, let $A'x' = b'$. Then $x'_i = x_i + \delta(x_i)$. If the relative size of $\delta(x_i)$ is large compared to the relative sizes of the $\delta(a_{ij})$ and $\delta(b_i)$ we call the system ill-conditioned. In an ill-conditioned system the solution is very sensitive to small changes in the coefficients. Another way of saying this is that an uncertainty in the coefficients will be greatly amplified in the solution. Such uncertainty exists, for example, if the coefficients are the results of measurements. Even if the matrix A is exactly given, a perturbation will result when the a_{ij} are put in floating point form.

An excellent discussion of condition and scaling is given by Forsythe and Moler (1967). We shall only point out here that the condition of a system can be improved by scaling, although what is the best way is still an open question. The simplest scaling is the following: find

$$s_i = \max_j |a_{ij}| , \qquad i = 1(1)n ,$$

and divide the ith equation by s_i, and repeat this for each stage. However, it is easy to see that it is not necessary to actually do the scaling. Suppose that after scaling no interchange is necessary (this can be arranged by interchanging first). Then

$$a_{ij}^{(2)} = \frac{a_{ij}}{s_i} - \left(\frac{a_{i1}s_1}{a_{11}s_i}\right)\frac{a_{1j}}{s_1} = \frac{a_{ij}}{s_i} - \frac{a_{i1}}{a_{11}}\frac{a_{1j}}{s_i} ,$$

so that row scaling cannot affect the relative size of a_{ij} and $m_{i1}a_{1j}$. Row scaling only affects the choice of pivotal element.

7.4 THE FULL ALGORITHM

In the Gaussian elimination algorithm which follows we have made one change in the pivoting procedure. Instead of actually interchanging rows, we simply relabel the rows. The quantities $p(i)$ will be the new row indices.

For $k = 1(1)n$
- $p(k) = k$,

(7.4–1) For $k = 1(1)n - 1$,
- For $i = k + 1(1)n$
  - $s_i = \max\limits_{j \geq k} |a_{p(i),j}|$.
- Find i^* such that

$$\frac{|a_{p(i^*),k}|}{s_i^*} = \max_{i \geq k} \frac{|a_{p(i),k}|}{s_i}$$

- $r = p(k)$
- $p(k) = p(i^*)$
- $p(i^*) = r$,
- For $i = k + 1(1)n$
  - $a_{p(i),k} = \dfrac{a_{p(i),k}}{a_{p(k),k}}$,
  - For $j = k + 1(1)n$
    - $a_{p(i),j} = a_{p(i),j} - a_{p(i),k}a_{p(k),j}$.

Now, when we compute new right hand sides and solve for the x_j, the row index i is replaced by $p(i)$.

(7.4–2)
$$\begin{aligned}&\text{For } k = 1(1)n-1,\\&\quad \text{For } i = k+1(1)n\\&\quad\quad b_{p(i)} = b_{p(i)} - a_{p(i),k}b_{p(k)}\,.\end{aligned}$$

(7.4–3)
$$\begin{aligned}&\text{For } k = 1(1)n\\&\quad i = n-k+1\\&\quad x_i = [a_{p(i),i}]^{-1}\left[b_{p(i)} - \sum_{j=i+1}^{n} a_{p(i),j}x_j\right].\end{aligned}$$

When these algorithms are turned into programs, safeguards against division by zero, underflow, and overflow have to be included.

Finally, Forsythe and Moler (1967), and Wilkinson [in Ralston and Wilf (1967)] discuss a method for improving the accuracy of the solution of a linear system called *iterative* improvement. Let $x^{(1)}$ be the solution of $Ax = b$ obtained by Gaussian elimination. Let

$$r^{(1)} = b - Ax^{(1)}\,.$$

Let $x^{(2)}$ be the solution of $Ax = r^{(1)}$, and let

$$r^{(2)} = r^{(1)} - Ax^{(2)}\,,$$

and so on. Then if $x = x^{(1)} + x^{(2)} + \cdots$,

$$\begin{aligned}Ax &= Ax^{(1)} + Ax^{(2)} + \cdots\\&= b - r^{(1)} + r^{(1)} - r^{(2)} + \cdots\,.\end{aligned}$$

The vectors $r^{(i)}$ are called residuals and presumably get small as $i \to \infty$. If iterative improvement is used, it is essential that double precision arithmetic be used to compute the $r^{(i)}$. The attractive thing about iterative improvement is that (7.4–1) does not have to be repeated, only (7.4–2) and (7.4–3) with b replaced by $r^{(i)}$.

EXERCISES

Section 7.1

1. Find the exact number of multiplications or divisions required to find the solution of a linear system.

Section 7.2

2. Find a specific 2×2 system like (7.2–1) which will have the indicated behavior. Assume a machine with a five decimal digit fractional part.
3. Write an algorithm for solving a linear system by complete pivoting.

Section 7.4

4. Write a program to solve an $n \times n$ linear system by the algorithms given in this section.

BIBLIOGRAPHY AND AUTHOR INDEX

Numbers following each entry are page references.

CODDINGTON, E. A., and N. LEVINSON (1955), *Theory of Ordinary Differential Equations*, New York: McGraw-Hill. (40)

DAVIS, MARTIN (1958), *Computability and Unsolvability*, New York: McGraw-Hill. (10)

DAVIS, PHILIP J. (1965), *Interpolation and Approximation*, New York: Blaisdell. (71, 86, 97)

FORSYTHE, GEORGE, and CLEVE B. MOLER (1967), *Computer Solution of Linear Algebraic Systems*, Englewood Cliffs, N. J.: Prentice-Hall. (109, 111, 113)

HENRICI, P. (1962a), *Discrete Variable Methods in Ordinary Differential Equations*, New York: Wiley. (40, 43, 48, 94)

HENRICI, P. (1962b), *Error Propagation for Difference Methods*, New York: Wiley. (94)

HILDEBRAND, F. B. (1956), *Introduction to Numerical Analysis*, New York: McGraw-Hill. (59, 78)

INCE, E. L., (1944), *Ordinary Differential Equations*, New York: Dover. (43)

MOORE, R. E. (1966), *Interval Analysis*, Englewood Cliffs, N. J.: Prentice-Hall. (13)

OSTROWSKI, A. M. (1960), *Solution of Equations and Systems of Equations*, New York: Academic Press. (93)

RALSTON, ANTHONY (1965), *A First Course in Numerical Analysis*, New York: McGraw-Hill. (50, 52, 78, 85)

RALSTON, A., and H. S. WILF (1967), *Mathematical Methods for Digital Computers, V. II*, New York: Wiley. (113)

RICE, J. R. (1964), *The Approximation of Functions*, Reading, Massachusetts: Addison-Wesley. (97)

TRAUB, J. F. (1961), *Iterative Methods for the Solution of Equations*, Englewood Cliffs, N. J.: Prentice-Hall. (93)

WENDROFF, BURTON (1966), *Theoretical Numerical Analysis*, New York: Academic Press. (85, 95, 98, 110, 111)

WILKINSON, J. H. (1963), *Rounding Errors in Algebraic Processes*, Englewood Cliffs, N. J.: Prentice-Hall. (13)

SUBJECT INDEX

ABCDE69